EXPLORING WALES

EXPLORING WALES

Malcolm Joyce

Series Editor: Tom Lawton

WARD LOCK

A WARD LOCK BOOK

First published in the UK 1998
by Ward Lock
Wellington House
125 Strand
London
WC2R 0BB

A Cassell Imprint
First paperback edition 1999

A British Library Cataloguing in Publication Data block for this book may
be obtained from the British Library.

ISBN 0-7063-7737-0

Printed and bound in Slovenia by DELO-Tiskana by arrangement with
Korotan, d.o.o., Ljubljana

Contents

Foreword

Wales is a land of myths, legends and folk tales; of dwarves, giants, gnomes, fairies and even dragons (reflected in its national emblem); of mysterious places where magic abounds, or so the story books would have us believe. More certainly, Wales is a land of outstanding natural beauty, of mountains soaring high into the skies above and fast-flowing streams impatiently cascading over boulder-strewn beds, seemingly eager to deposit their transient contents into a myriad of secluded, tranquil lakes nestling below. It is also a land of vast open spaces, of sweet, airy, deciduous woodlands and more foreboding, dense, darker coniferous forests; a land richly embellished with magnificent coastal scenery where high, precipitous cliffs plunge steeply into swirling seas far below and rocky, raking headlands separate and shelter numerous coves and glistening beaches covered with golden sands.

This unique land is host to no less than three national parks, which spread across the countryside in Snowdonia, the Brecon Beacons and along the Pembrokeshire Coast. These regions are perfect for exploring on foot, and Malcolm Joyce's timely addition to the *Exploring* series of innovative walking guidebooks, *Exploring Wales*, does just this in describing 20 superb walking routes through the majestic Welsh countryside.

The author is a scientist by training and his meticulously researched and presented route directions reflect this background, never leaving the reader in the slightest doubt as to where they should place their next steps, even when crossing the most challenging terrain in extremes of weather! Happily, this crisp, precise analysis is peppered with interesting facts and penetrating insights about the many places visited, providing fascinating glimpses into Welsh history and the industrial heritage which is still much in evidence today.

Malcolm is also an accomplished landscape photographer and his impressive pictures selected for the book not only illustrate and assist in route-finding, but also present irresistible reference for walkers to look back at time and again in recalling their own happy times spent exploring this mountainous land.

I have had the pleasure of walking with Malcolm in these three national parks and, more dubiously, of trying to keep pace with him! May I commend that you do likewise, setting out well prepared and at a walking pace which you find comfortable, taking appropriate care, enjoying yourself to the full and standing on spots that will release emotions that have to be experienced for yourselves, not described in books.

May my own good wishes accompany your explorations in these walker-friendly lands of the red dragon.

TOM LAWTON
Series Editor

Introduction

There is something almost inexplicable about walking in Wales. For me, my years of *Exploring Wales* have provided a rich and vast array of memories, experiences and perspectives. I have danced along the tops of the Glyderau in blistering August sunshine, with my ears and shoulders burnt raw. I have clambered up Pen yr Ole Wen in sheets of horizontal rain. I have wandered in blizzards among the Carneddau and strolled through Welsh forestry with my nose tantalized by the priceless air. I have scaled the glassy challenges of a frozen Bristly Ridge and gazed at the cloudless sky above the Rhinogyll, wondering how such an immense landscape could provide such variety. I have climbed the dusty tracks aloft Pen y Fan and roamed the winter wonderland of the Berwyns.

All these memories draw me back time and again to the countryside of Wales. I find that I forget the torrential rain, the blisters, the stale sandwiches, melted Mars bars and lukewarm flask-tea, the soggy feet, the cunning midges, the wind that penetrates anything, the sore shoulders and the never-ending ascent! To stroll across the Arans, or to gaze at the Strumble Head lighthouse, banishes any recollections of the effort involved.

The Welsh countryside is blessed with superlative natural features, such as the Nant Ffrancon or Ramsey Island, but it also has a rich historical and folk heritage. The Penrhyn slate tips or the lime kilns of Porthclais are examples of the country's industrial heritage, while there are numerous myths and legends concerning the time spent in Wales by such infamous characters as Owain Glyndwr and King Arthur. More recent history abounds, too; there is much evidence of the World War impact on the landscape of Wales, everything from twisted aircraft wreckage to initials carved on a derelict look-out post. Much of the country's history tells of past desperate times while some of it, regretfully, harks back to a time when the landscape was taken for granted and irreversibly abused. Hence, it is important that we take care now to respect and preserve this heritage, whether natural or historical. This may be done by supporting conservation work and the National Park Authorities or, more simply, by following the Country Code and picking up the odd piece of litter when we see it. If this book encourages readers to get out there and explore Wales for themselves, then its objective will have been achieved.

Acknowledgements

A number of people deserve a specific mention for their valuable input to this book. In particular, I am grateful for the company and expert assistance of Geoff and Asuncion Garnham, the Lawton family, Orla McGinnis, Charlie and Sian Price, the Simpson family, Deborah Smith, Steve Stanaway, Adrian Vann and, of course, Johnny Walker.

I am forever indebted to Pete and Ruth Joyce for introducing me to mountaineering when I was too young to know better, and to Tom Lawton for providing the opportunity to compile this work. His continual assistance, guidance, proofreading and advice (plus photographs!) have been invaluable.

The text has been checked by the relevant National Park Authorities of Snowdonia, the Brecon Beacons and the Pembrokeshire Coast. Their help and suggestions have been invaluable.

Finally, I am heavily indebted to Michelle, who has put up with me, Moel Siabod and the endless evenings spent typing, examining photographs and cleaning boots.

Using the Book

This book covers 20 walking routes in Wales, based in and around the national parks of Snowdonia, the Brecon Beacons and Pembrokeshire. Each route is described in detail, with full directions and gradients, plus descriptions of the scenery encountered on the walk. Most of the routes are circular, however, in some cases the relief of the land making linear routes more appropriate; the route in the Preseli Hills and sections of the Nantlle Ridge are examples of this.

Each route is supported by a plan map of the walk, together with a cross-sectional relief diagram that illustrates the variation of the gradient along the route. The walks are also illustrated by photographs of particular features of interest.

Arrangement

The 20 routes are arranged in respect of their geography, from north to south, in seven sections. As far as possible, the walks have been distributed evenly across Wales. However, particular areas of interest – principally Snowdonia and the Pembrokeshire Coast – inevitably include the greatest proportion of routes.

Summary tables

Each route is summarized in an introductory table that includes details of the starting location(s), car parking and public transport, specific features of interest and an assessment of the footpaths and terrain in general. Each walk is also attributed a grading of *easy*, *moderate* or *difficult*, and an overall time allowance. Finally, details are provided of the distance covered, total height gained and the principal heights included in the walk.

GRADING

The grading of each walk provides the reader with an idea of the suitability of the route for themselves and their party in terms of length, terrain, any tricky navigational sections or complications due to the weather and seasonal variations. The grading also takes into account any treacherous sections of the route. The table overleaf shows typical statistical details of the three grades.

Easy routes can normally be attempted by any member of the family who is of average fitness. These routes are usually short and because of this are often suitable for half-day excursions or for days of relatively poor weather. The ascents included in any easy route are nominal and there should be few, if any, treacherous sections. Since the navigational expertise required is elementary, they are also ideal for learning about map reading. Much of the route will also follow established paths and bridleways. Easy routes are not severely complicated by poor weather, although do remember to take standard equipment such as map, compass, waterproofs, spare food and warm clothing with you.

Moderate routes are usually longer than easy routes and in some cases might take up a whole day. There will be several moderate ascents but nothing too steep, exposed or exacting; the associated navigation requires thought but the paths are adequate. Always review the members of your party at the start, taking the length and nature of the walk into consideration – some moderate routes will be too long and strenuous for small children. There may also be a few sections that could be dangerous, so youngsters will need restraining.

WALK LOCATIONS

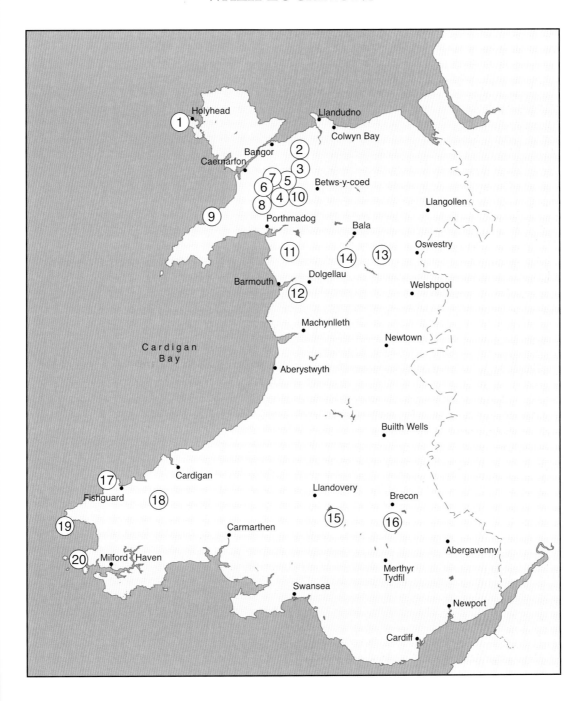

CHARACTERISTIC	EASY ROUTES		MODERATE ROUTES		DIFFICULT ROUTES	
	FROM	TO	FROM	TO	FROM	TO
Walking time hours	4	5½	4	6½	5	7½
Walking distance kilometres miles	9 5.6	14.5 9.1	9.25 5.8	20 12.5	9 5.6	17 10.6
Total height gained metres feet	120 394	827 2,713	213 699	1,028 3,372	865 2,837	1,237 4,057
Highest peak metres feet	0 (0)	827 (2,688)	0 (0)	905 (2,907)	677 (2,222)	1,085 (3,560)

Difficult routes combine the extremes of length and physical exertion. These routes are best attempted in favourable weather by experienced walkers who are well equipped. There will often be sections of sheer drops and exposure, while some of the climbs will require elementary scrambling skills. Difficult routes are therefore not recommended for children. They have added complication of being completely transformed in winter and under these conditions will test the stamina of the fittest walkers. Because of this, additional equipment is essential – make sure you are kitted out with ice-axe, crampons and substantial windproof winter clothing. Learn how to use the equipment and take extra food with you, allowing more time for the walk than you would in the summer months. Further essential items include a torch, whistle, hat and gloves, and a survival bag.

STATISTICS

All statistics for each route – time allowance, distance and total height gained – are calculated from the relevant Ordnance Survey map. The distance is calculated using the scale of the map while the total height gained is determined from the relief diagram of the route, making use of the contour lines, with each route starting from sea level. The time allowance is calculated assuming an average walker's pace, with the severity of the terrain included using the contour lines once more. There is usually one rest per walk.

Abbreviations

The following abbreviations have been used in the route descriptions:

L	left	W	west, western, westerly
R	right		
N	north, northern, northerly	WNW	west north west
		NW	north west
NNE	north north east	NNW	north north west
NE	north east	m	metre(s)
ENE	east north east	ft	feet
E	east, eastern, easterly	km	kilometre(s)
		yd	yard(s)
ESE	east south east		
SE	south east	OS	Ordnance Survey
SSE	south south east		
S	south, southern, southerly	OLM	Ordnance Survey Outdoor Leisure map
SSW	south south west		
SW	south west		
WSW	west south west		

OSLR	Ordnance Survey Landranger map	L-STILE	ladder stile
		P-STILE	post stile
OSPF	Ordnance Survey Pathfinder map	RSPB	Royal Society for the Protection of Birds
MR	map reference	RNLI	Royal National Lifeboat Institution
K-GATE	kissing gate		

RECORDED HEIGHTS

The metric conversion for the heights included in the routes has been taken from the Ordnance Survey maps and is supplemented with the imperial equivalent given by the conversion 1 metre = 3.281 feet.

Maps and Compass

The appropriate map(s) and a reliable compass are essential – even for the easy routes. Consulting your map and compass frequently and correctly will assist in reliable route-finding along the walks.

ORDNANCE SURVEY MAPS

Ordnance Survey Outdoor Leisure Maps are recommended for most of the walks. However, in some cases the relevant Ordnance Survey Landranger or Pathfinder Maps should be used instead: details are given in the summary table at the start of each route description. The Ordnance Survey maps are excellent guides to all the areas featured but are not infallible since features on the

Sheep crofts form a maze in the snow.

ground change, for example paths may cross fields differently and stiles are replaced or relocated. In these instances you should proceed with confidence to the next feature given in the text. Apparent differences noticed by the author have been noted in the route descriptions.

COMPASS BEARINGS

Most compass bearings in the route descriptions are given to the nearest 22.5° point, i.e. N, NNE, NE, etc. This is usually accurate enough due to the short distances between successive bearings and the accompanying definition of the path. However, there are many sheer drops and treacherous clifftops in Wales, especially in Snowdonia, and you must therefore study your map and compass carefully when visibility is restricted by poor weather. In instances where accurate navigation is required, across moorland, for example, specific numerate bearings are given to the nearest degree.

Safety

When planning any walk, safety always comes first. A simple misplaced footstep can result in a night's stay in hostile, life-threatening conditions, so it is important that you plan for all eventualities and always go prepared.

When you have decided which route you would like to take, let someone know and give them an approximate time of return. Make sure you take the correct equipment for both the weather conditions and type of walk you are attempting: the walk gradings will help you with this. In general, you should dress appropriately for the season and always take spare warm clothes in case you or a member of your party gets cold or is forced to wait for the help of the emergency services (Mountain Rescue 999). Remember to wear a warm hat and gloves in winter and a sun hat in summer – sun-stroke is unpleasant and can be serious. Make sure that each member of the party has adequate wet-weather gear since conditions can change swiftly, even in high summer. It is also important to take enough food and drink for the route and, as well, some spare rations for

Snowdon viewed across the disused quarries of Cwm Llan.

emergencies; sweets, biscuits, chocolate, glucose tablets and carbohydrate drinks are popular. It is worthwhile carrying a first aid kit consisting of a few plasters and dressings, painkillers, antiseptic cream and sun cream – this will prove invaluable against the misery of blisters, insect bites, cuts, grazes and sunburn.

Many emergencies result from getting lost and can be avoided. Take the right map, know how to use your compass and be sensible about what you attempt! It is crucial that you take a torch and whistle with you, especially if walking alone, so that you can signal your position in emergencies at night: the emergency signal is six short bursts on the whistle or six flashes of the torch. If you are

Useful Welsh words

aber	mouth of river
afon	river
allt	hill, cliff, wood
bach	little, small
bae	bay
bedd	grave, tomb, sepulchre
bera	pyramid
betws	oratory, chapel, birch grove
blaen	front, first, edge
braich,	
breichiau	branch, headland
bryn	hill
bwlch	pass, saddle
bychau	little, small
cadair	chair
caer	wall, castle, city
capel	chapel
carn	cairn, pile of stones
castell	castle
celyn	holly
cilfach	nook, creek, bay
clogwyn	cliff, crag, precipice
coed	wood, trees
craig	rock
crib	comb, crest, ridge
cwm	valley, corrie
cyfrwy	saddle
cyhoeddus	public
Cymru	Wales
daear	earth, ground
du	black
eglwys	church
eilio	weave, plait
esgair	ridge
ffordd	way, road
ffrwd	stream, torrent
ffynnon	well, spring
gwern	meadow
gwynt	wind
hebog	hawk, falcon
hosan	stocking
llan	church, village
llydaw	Brittany
llyn	lake, pond, pool
maes	field
mawr	big, great, large
morfa	moor, fen, marsh
mynydd	mountain
mynydd-dir	hill country
nant	brook, gorge, ravine
pant	hollow, valley
parc	park
pont	bridge, arch
pwll	pit, pool, pond
rhos	moon, heath, plain
rhyd	ford
saeth	arrows
sych	dry
trum	ridge
twyn	hill, hillock, knoll
tyle	slope, hill
ynys	island

walking in a group and someone in the party is injured, define the position of the casualty as accurately as possible on the map and then go for help. If there are enough of you, leave someone with the casualty. When you reach the emergency services they will need as much information as possible on the location of the casualty and the state and type of injuries sustained. You must then do as you are told and leave the rest to the experts.

Of course, the best solution is to avoid getting into difficulty in the first place and enjoy the routes in this book in safety.

Spelling

The spelling of place names and the names of mountains, hills, streams, rivers and so on often varies in mountainous areas and Wales is no exception. In some cases there can be three or more spellings of the same name due to changes in local dialect and the Welsh language. The names quoted in the route descriptions have been taken from the Ordnance Survey maps and the reader can expect some variation with those found on the ground.

Route 1: HOLYHEAD MOUNTAIN

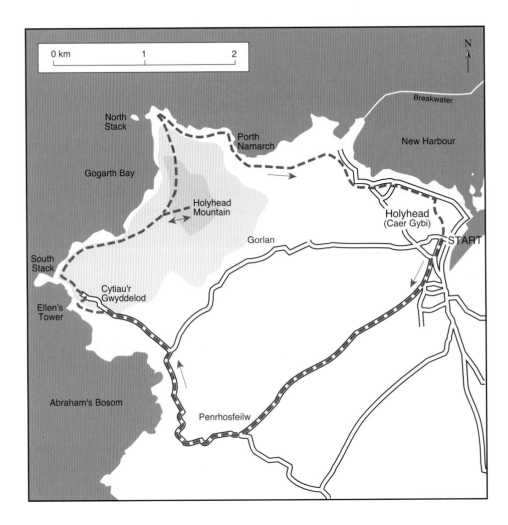

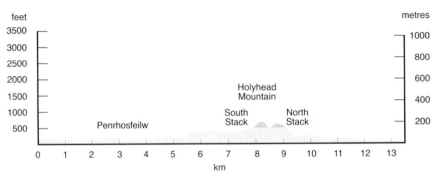

2

THE NORTH COAST AND ANGLESEY

Route 1 • Holyhead Mountain

STARTING LOCATION
Large car park in Holyhead centre (small charge).
OSLR 114 or OSPF 734/MR 245825.

ALTERNATIVE STARTING LOCATION
Elim Pentecostal church MR 246824 (no parking).

PUBLIC TRANSPORT
Bus routes to Holyhead (along the A5 (T) road).

OVERVIEW/INTEREST
Beautiful coastal walk on Anglesey.
Holyhead Mountain features splendid views and
    the Caer y Twr fort.
Points of interest include the standing stones at
    Penrhosfeilw, Ellen's Tower RSPB observation
    tower, South Stack lighthouse, the USAAF
    memorial and St Cybi's Church

FOOTPATHS
Sections of the route are on roads, so beware of
    occasional traffic.
Many dangerous drops along the coastline paths
    so keep hold of children in these areas.

GRADING   Easy
TIME ALLOWANCE   5 hours
DISTANCE
Excluding height 13.5km (8 miles)
TOTAL HEIGHT GAINED 388m (1,275ft)
PRINCIPAL HEIGHT
Holyhead Mountain 220m (722 ft)

The way to Penrhosfeilw   *Allow ¼ hour*

Park in the long-stay car park near to the
pedestrianized centre of Holyhead and then find
the large decorative anchor that marks the end of
this shopping area (MR 246824). From this
position walk due W up the hill for a few paces,
taking the first turning on the L just before the
Elim Pentecostal church and the Anglesey Book
Shop. Holyhead is a bustling little town, usually
full of ferry-loads of tourists. Much of the traffic
has thankfully been kept to the lower reaches of
the town. As you head off SW, the noise rapidly
dies away and you are draped in quieter suburbs
of pebble-dashed houses. After a few hundred
paces the road forks and you should follow to the
R, keeping your SW bearing, along the road of
Maes Meilio. There are many new bungalows on
the L here, with a contrasting derelict barn on the
other side.

The houses become fewer as you progress and
the pavement ends, along with the bungalows.
These are replaced by some pretty allotments
against a backdrop of undulating open country
beyond. The road narrows but continues straight
on. You will pass a riding school on the R and might
see a few horses grazing nearby. There is a track
just after this, on the R, which should be
disregarded. Nature really takes over now, with the
ancient drystone walls reinforced by tangled
masses of brambles, bracken and gorse. At various

15

times of the year the yellow of the gorse is reflected along the verges which host a profusion of dandelions, daisies and buttercups, and you may spot a few butterflies hoisted by the sea breeze. The road climbs gently, past the occasional large bungalow, and views of Holyhead Mountain improve to the NW. To the SE views of Snowdonia are possible in clear weather.

About 2km (1¼ miles) from Holyhead you will reach the standing stones of Penrhosfeilw. These are set back in a meadow to the R, behind a barn and disused farm buildings. You can visit them via a black K-gate and there is also an information plaque. The standing stones are two tall slabs speckled with lichen, about 3m (10ft) tall and the same distance apart. Behind them, to the N, lies Holyhead Mountain. Their origin is uncertain but they are believed to be early Bronze Age (2000–1500 BC).

The way to Ellen's Tower and South Stack

Allow 1½ hours

From the standing stones, return to the road and continue SW. You will soon reach a wide, skewed T-junction where you should turn R to head due W. The lane descends gently among a few houses, towards a wide cove called Abraham's Bosom. After a few hundred paces the road begins to zigzag eccentrically, heading predominantly N towards Holyhead Mountain. This peak is small in comparison with its cousins in Snowdonia, but stands out impressively among the flat meadowlands of Anglesey as a ragged pile of boulders and steep cliffs.

The road ventures closer to the coast as it crosses Abraham's Bosom and reaches another T-junction (MR 216815), where you should turn L to head NW: this direction is signposted for South Stack (Ynys Lawd) and the RSPB. The road immediately crosses a stone bridge over a leafy tributary, which is followed by a small K-gate where a footpath leaves to the L. This path leads to a nearby beach and should be disregarded. The tarmac continues up an incline and an improved view of Holyhead Mountain is possible to the NNE.

A few hundred paces beyond this climb the road flattens and the terrain opens out as you approach the ancient settlement of Cytiau'r Gwyddelod, often referred to as the Ty Mawr hut circles. These lie among dense ferns to the R and can be reached via a stone stile. On the L opposite, there is a large car park. The settlement consists of numerous foundations, believed to be the remains of dwellings and workshops from around 500 BC to the post-Roman era.

To continue, cut across the car park and follow the signs for Ellen's Tower. This is a small castellated building on the edge of the cliffs just

south of South Stack and it is reached across the heather via a wide, distinct path. Ellen's Tower is the RSPB look-out post and information centre. It is well worth a visit, although you may have to dodge the crowds of keen bird-spotters who tend to congregate to spy on the inhabitants of the nearby cliffs! From Ellen's Tower there are spectacular views down on to South Stack and its lighthouse. This was built in 1809 and its light has a range of 45km (28 miles). Hoards of sea birds flock around it and the treacherous cliff-tops. Take particular care of children – there are some lethal exposed sections along the path here.

The way to Holyhead Mountain and back to Holyhead
Allow 2½ hours

Continue along the coast on the clear, dusty path. It joins the tarmac road again after a short, steep climb up from the RSPB centre. The road swings around to the w and there is sometimes an ice-cream van waiting here! Unfortunately, it is not possible to visit the lighthouse and the associated service road is cordoned off. The path heads off due N to follow the coast once more and climbs steeply.

The approach to Holyhead Mountain and Gogarth Bay.

As it follows the contours, it changes to head NE and views of Holyhead Mountain return. The path visits a derelict look-out post of some sort before heading due E for Holyhead Mountain proper. The large cove of Gogarth Bay appears to the N. Meanwhile you will notice several transmission dishes at the radio-relay station ahead. The path skirts to the R of this and begins to change course slightly to the NE. As you approach the peak ahead, you might notice the brightly coloured specks of climbers on the W cliffs. Disregard any paths that descend to the R (SE), along the base of the cliffs. Out at sea you may see the ferries cross as they head for Ireland. The path continues to be clear and wide.

By following the path you should find that you pass to the W of the main peak and reach a distinct crossroads of paths. To include the summit you should turn R here and head due E. The path is clear and it is only a short climb up to the tri-

Glorious bracken gives way to Porth Namarch and Holyhead Bay.

angulation point at the top of Holyhead Mountain. In clear weather the views are superlative. You can look out E across the harbour and along the breakwater. There is the industrious town of Holyhead and beyond this the gentle, fertile flatlands of Anglesey. If the weather is good you should be able to see the lofty peaks of Snowdonia to the SE and follow them out along the Lleyn Peninsula, to the characteristic shapes around Yr Eifl. Anglesey often escapes the poorer weather that can haunt Snowdonia, so you may find you are a lucky spectator of a storm from afar.

The summit of Holyhead Mountain holds greater interest than just that provided by its views. It is the site of an ancient fort named Caer y Twr, which was possibly a Roman stronghold although its origin is uncertain. The remains consist of a long single rampart around the summit that is clearly identifiable from aerial photographs. Close to the summit there are the ruins of a Roman watch-tower.

You should rejoin the path by retracing your route of ascent (due W) and head off due N to the R. There is a short uphill scramble across a few derelict drystone walls before this section of the route descends quickly, and after a few hundred paces over heather and loose rocks you will reach the high ground above North Stack (Ynys Arw) and the fog signal station. The views from North Stack are pleasant and as you look across the ocean panorama you may see an occasional ferry. Do not descend from the high ground to the signal station; instead, follow the coastal path that heads off SE, keeping the cliffs a few hundred paces to your L. This path is wide and is used by vehicles to service the signal station. It descends gently and passes the extensive Breakwater Quarries to the R. In this section it is sandy and smooth, bordered by large clumps of gorse and other dense vegetation, while the coast follows to the L. About 1km (⅝ mile) from North Stack the path ends in a new gate and K-gate.

Immediately after the gates there is a memorial to the eight men killed in 1944 in the air crash at North Stack in a B-29 USAAF bomber. The memorial includes a section of the propeller from the wreckage. The path is resumed by a road of smooth tarmac and the country park area of the North Stack region opens out to the R. Within a few hundred metres you will reach a T-junction, where you should turn L; there is a derelict cottage opposite. You are now heading ENE. The route follows the line of the disused tramway from the quarries and is consequently very straight. You pass under several disused bridges and over a cattle grid as you descend into a shallow cutting. Keep an eye open for the numerous wild flowers on the banks to either side; in addition to dandelions, buttercups and daisies, there is the occasional wild iris to be spotted.

After a few hundred paces the cutting opens out and you approach the harbour and the suburbs of Holyhead. There are many boats on your L, both swaying with the tide and in dry dock. You will pass a large pub, the Boathouse Hotel, also to the L, and should keep to the pavement near to the houses on the R. A large grass verge develops to the L. Disregard the first two turnings to the R, which lead into the residential area of the town, and take the third. This junction is distinguished at present by burgundy-red railings that run along the pavement for a short distance, and also by the Holyhead Boatyard opposite. By following this road you will head into the centre of Holyhead.

Holyhead is a busy harbour town and has much to offer with good pubs, restaurants and shops. Of particular interest, and worth a visit, is the Caer Gybi Roman fort in the centre of the town, near to the inner harbour. This fort is believed to be the site of a sixth-century Christian monastic foundation. The medieval St Cybi's church was built in the thirteenth century and rebuilt in the fifteenth and sixteenth. The surrounding wall is of Roman origin and is very well preserved, although it can be obscured by the encroaching modern developments. It is possible that the fort was part of a network employed to deter Irish invaders and it may be associated with the larger fort on Holyhead Mountain.

Alternative routes

ESCAPES

Several short cuts are possible on this route. You can omit Holyhead Mountain and follow the path SW (MR 216828) along the base of the cliffs just beyond the radio transmitters. This meets with another path after about 500 paces and heads due E, bypassing the peak. After a further few hundred paces it reaches the small settlement of Gorlan and then follows the tarmac lane into Holyhead via Pont Hwfa. Otherwise, later in the route you can omit the North Stack and head off due W from the summit of Holyhead Mountain. This route rambles W for a few hundred paces before heading S into Gorlan and once again tracking W into Holyhead.

EXTENSIONS

There are no obvious extensions to the route as described.

Route 2: THE COASTAL CARNEDDAU & ABER FALLS

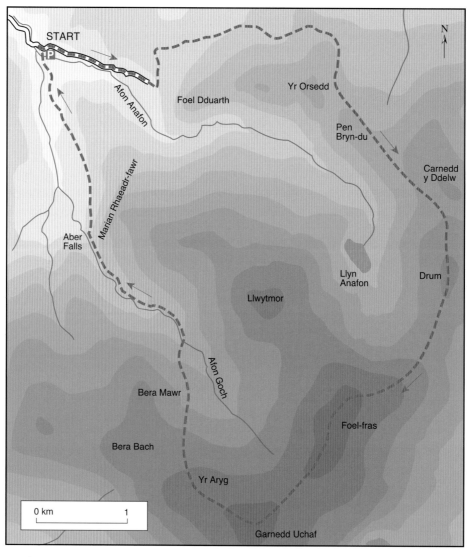

START

P

N

Afon Anafon

Foel Dduarth

Yr Orsedd

Pen Bryn-du

Carnedd y Ddelw

Marian Rhaeadr-fawr

Aber Falls

Llyn Anafon

Drum

Llwytmor

Afon Goch

Bera Mawr

Foel-fras

Bera Bach

Yr Aryg

Garnedd Uchaf

0 km   1

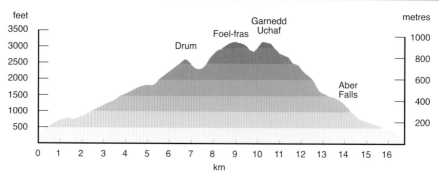

feet | metres

3500   1000
3000
2500   800
2000   600
1500
1000   400
500   200

Drum   Foel-fras   Garnedd Uchaf   Aber Falls

0 1 2 3 4 5 6 7 8 9 10 11 12 13 14 15 16

km

Route 2 • The Coastal Carneddau and Aber Falls

STARTING LOCATION
Aber Falls car park(s).
OLM 17/MR 664719.
Capacity for 30 cars.
No toilets.

ALTERNATIVE STARTING LOCATION
None.

PUBLIC TRANSPORT
Bus route Conwy–Bangor (along the A55 road).

OVERVIEW/INTEREST
A combined coastal and high-level route, which
   includes several peaks of NE Snowdonia.
Gentle, uncomplicated ridge walking contrasts
   with quiet forest paths.
Views of the valley of Aber and the unusual
   skeletal peaks of Bera Bach and Bera Mawr.
Features include Aber Falls, ancient settlements
   and the pretty river of the Afon Goch.

FOOTPATHS
Route is very clear for the first half of the walk.
Wide, grassy ridges require careful use of the
   compass in poor visibility.
Later sections involve navigation and careful
   route-finding.
Screes and short exposed areas must be crossed
   towards the end of the route.

GRADING   Difficult
TIME ALLOWANCE   7 hours
DISTANCE
Excluding height 17km (10.6 miles)
TOTAL HEIGHT GAINED 1,008m (3,326ft)
PRINCIPAL HEIGHTS
Drum 760m (2,526ft)
Foel-fras 942m (3,091ft)
Garnedd Uchaf 926m (3,038ft)

The way to Drum
Allow 2 hours

The car park that serves the popular tourist attraction of Aber Falls is divided by the Afon Aber. In the height of summer you may find you will have to persevere to find a suitable place to park by driving over the river via the hump-backed bridge and turning immediate R, where an additional area is set aside. The car park is set in the depths of deciduous forest and is sheltered, allowing you to prepare in seclusion for the walk ahead.

From the car park, walk over the hump-backed bridge if necessary and continue past a small, pretty cottage on the L, walking up the narrow, tarmac lane. The road climbs steeply and there is very little time to acclimatize to the gradient. After about 500 paces, you will pass a farmhouse on the R and a variety of farm buildings and machinery on the L. The shelter of the forest slowly depletes, only remaining on the L side at this stage. The sides of the road are bordered by dense nettles and ferns on the verges, above which stand tall hedges of hawthorn. Over and beyond this vegetation the crowded mass of peaks that comprise the Carneddau and Glyderau can be seen to the S.

The climb continues relentlessly for at least 1km (⅝ mile) and the valley occupied by the Afon Anafon will open up gradually to the R. You should be able to hear the river far below you, and a few paces further on you will encounter more farm buildings on both sides of the road. The road is reasonably quiet, but do not be complacent because the gradient is steep and traffic can pass at speed. The deciduous forest of the lower slopes returns slightly at this stage in the form of very large oak trees, particularly on the R. These trees almost coincide with several electricity pylons of similar height as the road passes under the associated power lines. At this stage you will pass a metal gate on the R bearing a sign reading 'No sheep'. Disregard the path served by this and continue along the tarmac road. After the gate, drystone walls replace the hedges on both sides and, about 20 paces further on, another path leaves over the drystone wall on the left and is waymarked with a yellow arrow. Disregard this path and continue on the tarmac road, which continues to climb! The view to the s is now more developed and the distinctive, knobbly peaks of Bera Bach and Bera Mawr are visible. These peaks are quite eerie in appearance since their predominantly smooth, grassy lower slopes are decorated by symmetrical, angular outcrops of grey rock.

After a further 200 paces or so and a slight turn to the E the tarmac ends, and is replaced by dusty, rock-strewn terrain. Immediately there is a metal gate with a sign hung over it: 'Dim parcio' (no parking). The trail changes dramatically here and is very rugged. Pass through the gate and follow the lower path, which after about 200 paces meets up with a tall, cemented wall on the L. You are now heading due N, away from the large spur of Foel Dduarth. This spur is the most W end of the ridge which the route eventually scales. However, for the next kilometre or so the route ventures to the N of the ridge to allow the coast to be viewed and enjoyed. The rock-strewn track is wide and there is evidence of farm-vehicle use in the form of the deep grooves worn by heavy tyres. The track heads N until the coast beyond can be seen, at which point it turns sharp R to head E, following in the direction of the pylons.

The views to the coast are unusual for a walk in Snowdonia, since such sights are often only possible when considerable altitude is achieved. In this case, however, the view out towards Penmaenmawr and the Conwy estuary is un-interrupted and impressive in fine weather. A short distance beyond the coast two islands can be seen. The smaller of the two, which is visible in its entirety, is called 'Priestholm' or Puffin Island, while the peninsula to the L of this is the E extent of Anglesey. The names of Priestholm and Puffin Island attributed to the smaller island have origins that are centuries apart. 'Priestholm' comes from the Norse Christians who inhabited Anglesey in the sixth century. These settlers were devoted to St Seiriol, who constructed a small religious cell on Priestholm. 'Puffin Island' is a much later English

name, earned from the abundance of puffins found there to this day.

The terrain which the path crosses is now flat and windswept by the coastal breeze. The sheep in this area have taken to sheltering from the elements under small boulders, which they burrow beneath to leave them partially exposed across the mountainside. You will need to ford a few small streams that trickle across the path in places, while in the medium ground ahead a large square enclosure made from drystone walls comes into view. The ridge on the R rises gracefully while to the L the pylons, ugly in comparison, follow the path closely into the distance. The path meanders back and forth as a grey trail and is unmistakable at this stage.

Beyond the square enclosure (MR 682722) the path begins to climb steadily and becomes wetter, with several small streams crossing it within a few hundred paces. As you come over the slight rise ahead the view towards Conwy opens up rapidly, and Foel Lwyd dominates to the E. This is a lumpy hill that is scarred by quarries and the associated waste tips, especially on its S side. About 100 paces after reaching the slight rise in the route, there is a crossroads of paths. The one to the L is waymarked as the 'North Wales Path' and heads N towards the coast and Llanfairfechan. The route ahead continues E towards Foel Lwyd, and is the Roman road leading immediately to Rowen and eventually to the Conwy valley. Disregard these two paths in favour of the route to the R, which climbs quickly to th E of the spur descending from Yr Orsedd. Once again, the path is clear, wide, rugged and rock strewn, making navigation easy. As the ascent progresses the path retains its definition, becoming more slate-ridden and loose.

In this area of Snowdonia a particular feature of interest is the small group of wild ponies which roams freely around the slopes of Drum and Drosgl, above the small reservoir of Llyn Anafon which lies at the base of the cwm directly to the W. They are a family group of various sizes, and there are usually a few foals among them. You may well be startled by their shrill whinnies that echo across the valley, as they are well camouflaged against the bracken and grass by their russet coats and flowing manes.

22

After a few hundred paces you will reach the top of the ridge and pass between the peaks of Pen Bryn-du to the W and Carnedd y Ddelw to the E. These are high points along the ridge of 557m (1,828ft) and 688m (2,257ft) respectively and are served by narrow footpaths, should you feel like including them along the way. Otherwise, the present track descends slightly to skirt the western slope of Carnedd y Ddelw. A vast panorama now dominates the view to the S, which is a crowded and confused array of peaks. Closest are the peaks situated along the ridge: Drum (760m 2,526ft), Foel–fras (942m 3,091ft) and Garnedd Uchaf (926m 3,038ft). Looking W are some characteristic, knobbly peaks with substantial outcrops of rock forming their summits. These appear to be in line but are actually at varying distances from you, and are (from S to N) Yr Aryg (865m 2,838ft), Bera Bach (807m 2,618ft) and Bera Mawr (794m 2,605ft). Beyond these are the lofty peaks of the Carneddau and Yr Elen, with the peaks of the W side of the Nant Ffrancon providing the background. The view to the NW improves as the route progresses and consists of the beautiful, sweeping cwm carved by Afon Anafon, which is apparently blocked by a dense mixture of coniferous and deciduous forest in the distance. The W side of the cwm is made up of the long E slopes of Llwytmor and Llwytmor Bach, while the reservoir of Llyn Anafon shimmers almost 1km (⅝ mile) away, at the base of the cwm.

After dividing, the path continues for a short distance before consolidating again. It is noticeably more eroded and has 'slipped' a short distance down the hillside, to expose dusty ground beneath the sparse vegetation. It develops into a steady climb and after a few hundred paces the ridge turns due S and gradually becomes wider. This has the effect of progressively obscuring the views to E and W as the gradient increases steadily. You might see more wild ponies on these slopes: they are quite tame and may be wondering what you are doing there too! After this gradual change of course from SE to due S, the path remains straight for about 0.5km (⅓ mile) and you will pass small cairns on both sides. You will be joined by a fence on the L and, as the gradient reduces, you will reach the

dome-shaped summit of Drum. There is a substantial drystone shelter just to the E of the fence which is reached by a P-stile.

The way to Foel-fras and Garnedd Uchaf

Allow 2 hours

From the summit of Drum the path continues to the S, gradually changing direction towards the W over a distance of about 2km (1¼ miles). The path leads away from the W side of the fence and proceeds effortlessly downhill, narrowing as the wide summit of Drum recedes. The ground is predominantly grass and is worn in places to expose the rocks and stones beneath. After several hundred paces of descent you will reach the flat saddle between Drum and Foel-fras, which is about 300m (325yd) long. This area is boggy and wet and the underlying peat is exposed in places, although the path itself remains comparatively dry. You will pass a P-stile over the fence on the L, which should be disregarded.

The ascent of the N shoulder of Foel-fras now begins and is a surprise; after the long steady climbs from Aber and to the summit of Drum, the ascent of Foel-fras can be sharp and may make your calf muscles ache! The ridge widens to about 100m (110yd) and hence the views are partially obscured, but the path is clear and the ground grassy and pleasant – not typical of terrain at almost 915m (3,000ft)! The fence to the L which has accompanied much of the ridge walking is crossed by an L-stile at this stage, after which it is replaced by a drystone wall (MR 700683) that continues to the summit of Foel-fras. Within 300m (325yd), on a bearing of SW, you should encounter a distinct change in terrain from lush grass to the peppered morass of rocks and boulders which make up the summit of Foel-fras. In clear weather you should be able to see the summit triangulation point from a distance. Foel-fras is a sharper peak than Drum and is completely different, being very rugged and completely free of vegetation throughout its 100m (110yd) radius.

The view from Foel-fras is expansive and includes the seaside resorts of Llandudno (NE),

23

together with its neighbouring hills of Great and Little Orme, and Conwy. The latter is significant because of the huge estuary – of the Afon Conwy – that extends to the N. Along the coast extending to the w of these areas are several other resorts, including Penmaenmawr and Llanfairfechan. You may also be able to see yachts and other vessels shimmering in the ocean beyond. It is a very peaceful panorama that is worth a few minutes' appreciation.

The way to Garnedd Uchaf continues ssw, gradually changing over a distance of 300m (325yd) to sw. Disregard the L-stile that lies about 100 paces SE of the Foel-fras summit and follow the drystone wall down. The route adopts a very gradual descent and quickly exchanges the rubble of Foel-fras for gentle ridge walking towards a shallow saddle. Unfortunately, the wall does not appear to be marked on the map; however, the path continues to be clear and substantial. The terrain consists of the peaty, eroded grassland encountered frequently on the lofty ridges of the Carneddau and in summer you will make swift progress along the dusty track, although the surrounding areas remain wet and boggy. As you progress and begin to climb, about 1km (⅝ mile) from the Foel-fras summit and looking s–N, the four distinctive peaks of Garnedd Uchaf, Yr Aryg, Bera Bach and Bera Mawr should appear. Continuing sw, you will rapidly reach the summit of Garnedd Uchaf which, at 926m (3,038ft), is only 30m (98ft) higher than the saddle.

In comparison with Foel-fras, Garnedd Uchaf has a spiky summit, once again a morass of boulders and smaller rocks but more jagged in relief, and similar to the famous outcrop of Castell y Gwynt to the sw of Glyder Fach. The views from Garnedd Uchaf are quite different from the gentle, smooth hillsides and coastal resorts admired earlier in the walk and support its position as a watershed for the drama of the Carneddau proper, to the s. Looking sw, the dominant feature is the steep-sided peak of Yr Elen (962m/3,157ft), which heads a ragged spur descending w towards Bethesda via the lesser peak of Foel Ganol. To the E of these is Foel Grach at 976m (3,202ft) and beyond is the giant Carnedd Llewelyn (1,064m/3,492ft). Behind this

impressive and unusual view of the Carneddau is Carnedd Dafydd, while the background is mainly of the characteristic w relief of the Nant Ffrancon.

The way to Yr Aryg and Aber Falls, and back through the forest   *Allow 3 hours*

From Garnedd Uchaf a distinct change in direction is required, to head NW towards the first knobbly peak of Yr Aryg, less than 1km (⅝ mile) away. The gradual descent loses height slowly and walking is easy and pleasant – fortunate at this stage of the walk! You are now crossing open country and the path is unclear. However, occasional sheep tracks should assist progress, while taking frequent compass bearings will ensure correct navigation. After a few hundred paces you will cross a bridlepath, which continues unfavourably WNW and should be disregarded. To the w the slate tips near Bethesda can be seen, possibly under a blue

haze on a summer afternoon, while in the distance to the NW are the Menai Straits and Anglesey. The terrain between Garnedd Uchaf and Yr Aryg can be quite wet and marshy, as indicated by the prevalence of spongy marsh plants and small boggy patches; trust the sheep tracks for a guide to dry areas! You will rapidly reach the outcrop of Yr Aryg, which is at about 865m (2,838ft) and appears larger than represented on the map. Again, it is a disordered pile of large boulders and rocks. You may wish to scramble up these to take in the view of Bera Bach, Bera Mawr and the sweeping valley of Cwm yr Afon Goch, which eventually leads to Aber Falls to the N. The large blocks of rock that comprise Yr Aryg provide a suitable shelter for the last mountain resting place of this route.

This walk does not include Bera Bach or Bera Mawr as peaks; however, they can easily be included as a small extension, after which you can rejoin the recommended descent. However, the author prefers the descent that is approximately parallel and to the E of these two peaks. This includes a pleasant section along the course of the Afon Goch, the river which forms from the drainage of the cwm that lies between the summits of Foel-fras and Garnedd Uchaf, to the NW. From Yr Aryg, you should head due N down the grassy slopes that lie opposite the rounded mass of Llwytmor. You will need to pick your way over the scattered rocks that lie N of Yr Aryg until, after about 200 paces, they give way to more grassy terrain. You may encounter more wild ponies on these gentle slopes, and boggy conditions will restrict your progress in places. After a few hundred paces, the gradient gradually increases and you will have fine views of the summits of Bera Bach and Bera Mawr on your L; they are made up of large stone blocks and resemble disordered ramparts from some angles. The direct translation of their names – the Large and Small

Delightful waterfalls of the Afon Goch.

Pyramid – is particularly appropriate, even if they are more untidy than the real thing!

As the gradient increases, you should notice more rocky outcrops among the grass and peat and will also need to cross some small tributaries. You should now alter your course, if necessary, very slightly to the E, because to continue N means crossing difficult, rocky terrain. The best idea is to follow the course of any substantial tributary, as these provide the easiest descent to the river below. The latter should now be in sight if the weather is clear. As you pick your way through the stubbly tussocks of grass, the company of small bubbling streams makes this descent particularly attractive. The rocky heights of Bera Mawr rise to your L and you should be able to see the more hostile N slopes that are neatly avoided by this route.

When you reach the Afon Goch, you will find a fast-flowing river of deep pools and small, boiling waterfalls. You should cross it where possible to gain the E side. This should not be difficult, since there is a variety of places where the water weaves in between large boulders that can be used as stepping stones even in torrential rain. On the E side of the river there is a selection of descending sheep tracks and you should follow one of these along the river bank for the next kilometre or so. As you progress along the river bank, the path will develop into a proper footpath at about MR 673693. The Afon Goch is a delightful watercourse with

Picking out a safe route on Marian Rhaeadr-fawr.

many small waterfalls and isolated pools; the grassy banks are perfect for a break should you wish to bathe those tired feet!

After about 1km (⅝ mile), you will pass some drystone sheepfolds on the same side of the river, followed after a few more paces by some ancient ruins. After these features the banks of the river steepen quickly and the path, still clear and free from rocks, rises above the river by several metres. The watercourse is quickly obscured by the deciduous trees that occupy the small gorge. These are mostly hawthorn and mountain ash and coincide with the path becoming looser because of shale pieces. The path descends more quickly as you approach Aber Falls. It negotiates the head of the falls deftly and is wet, even in dry weather, because of the poor drainage of the surrounding steep slopes. As you are at a considerable height above the river (the ground below remains obscured by trees), great care must be taken to avoid slipping on the wet slabs of rock that make up the path. Aber Falls descend around 100m (328ft) vertically, so you will hear them above the wind in the surrounding trees. The path is clear, if quite loose and slippery, and continues due N to the right side of the top of the falls as you approach them. This side of the falls is a very steep, flat slope known as Marian Rhaeadr-fawr.

The path traverses this slope and you should be able to see the screes of the lower half of Marian Rhaeadr-fawr and the coniferous forest beyond.

The traverse of Marian Rhaeadr-fawr is probably the most difficult section of this walk and can present problems for walkers with acute vertigo. Do not strain to see Aber Falls from your present position, as much better views are possible from further down the valley where it is safer, too. Beyond the watery rock-ledge the path leads very close to a large rowan tree, which is followed closely by a deep gully that partially divides the path. Do not be tempted by the descent down this rockfall, since it is not a path and is very dangerous and loose! Without surrendering height, you should pick your way around the head of the gully: the path is quite clear. This section is followed by several more rowan trees and another minor scramble over large rocks that obstruct the path. A wire fence will join you at this stage on the L to accompany you across the screes. There is a great deal of erosion in this area and the screes are subject to strict repair procedures, so you are guided carefully across them. Even so, the sandy terrain of small stone chips makes this a section of the route that requires some concentration, as it is also very steep. The path divides early in the traverse of the scree and you should take the upper path, losing no height. There are various notices referring to the erosion and providing some guidance. You should soon be able to see the L-stile ahead; this, thankfully, denotes the end of the scree and the beginning of the forest.

The L-stile is preceded by some ancient gateposts and followed by dense coniferous forest. The lofty trees provide some welcome shelter and the path is clear, soft and dry, It descends gently downhill along a similar gradient to that of the preceding screes. After about 500 paces you will approach a fork in the path accompanied by a sign denoting 'Historical feature' to the L, as denoted on the map at MR 668705. Whether to follow this sign is optional, since it introduces a small deviation in the route, but rejoins the forest path quickly further on. The feature is an ancient settlement situated amid tall ferns; there are a variety of hut circles in the lower regions of the Afon Rhaeadr-fawr and information is available at the Tourist Centre (MR 665713).

Proceeding along the main path you should pass a waymarker and then cross a fence using an L-stile, which has a large wooden gate to its R. The walker is thoughtfully protected from the barbed wire by rubber piping on the L-stile and you should pass another sign warning of erosion in the area. As you pass through the remains of a derelict drystone wall the forest clears to the L and Aber Falls are visible some distance to the S through a meadow of wild flowers and tall grasses. The forest on the R slowly changes to deciduous woods that are dominated by a few large oaks. After a few more paces, the path descends a short slope and joins a twin gravel track which is bordered by nettles on either side. At this stage there is a sign for the Tourist Centre, which is a short distance S along the gravel track and is recommended if time allows. Otherwise, continue along the track N for several hundred paces, disregarding a K-gate on the left. This will lead you to another K-gate over a footbridge and on to a tarmac road. The car park is situated a short distance along this road.

Alternative routes

ESCAPES
Other than returning via the outgoing route early in the walk, there are no suitable escape routes to be recommended.

EXTENSIONS
This route can be extended substantially in several ways. You can easily include the twin peaks of Bera Bach and Bera Mawr in the final descent (see route description). This necessitates a steep descent from the NE side of Bera Mawr to rejoin the recommended descent along the Afon Goch in the vicinity of the waterfalls, via Cwm yr Afon Goch (MR 668692).

The short extensions required to visit the foot of the falls and the Tourist Centre are strongly recommended; both are waymarked along the recommended route.

Route 3: THE CARNEDDAU AND YR ELEN

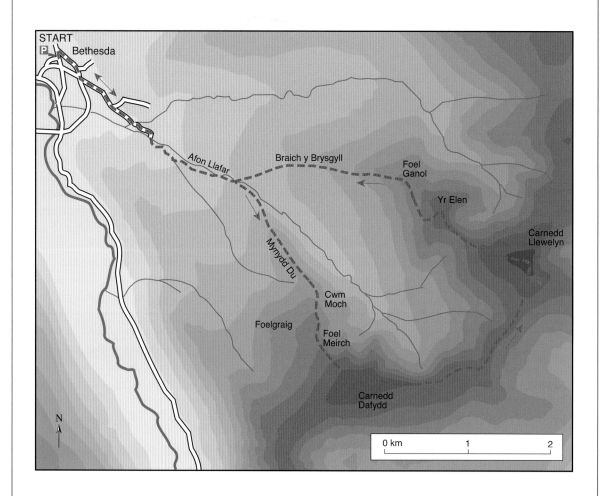

START
P Bethesda

Afon Llafar

Braich y Brysgyll

Foel Ganol

Yr Elen

Carnedd Llewelyn

Mynydd Du

Cwm Moch

Foelgraig

Foel Meirch

Carnedd Dafydd

N

0 km   1   2

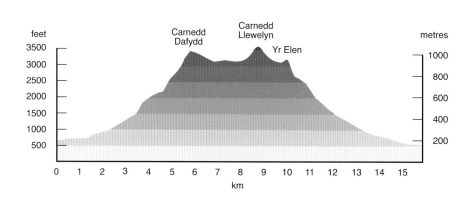

feet | metres

Carnedd Dafydd

Carnedd Llewelyn

Yr Elen

3500 — 1000
3000
2500 — 800
2000 — 600
1500
1000 — 400
500 — 200

0 1 2 3 4 5 6 7 8 9 10 11 12 13 14 15

km

Route 3 • The Carneddau and Yr Elen

STARTING LOCATION
Car park at Bethesda.
OLM 17/MR 623667.
Capacity for 25 cars.
Public toilets nearby.

ALTERNATIVE STARTING LOCATION
Near waterworks MR 637659 (no parking).

PUBLIC TRANSPORT
Bus route Bangor–Betws-y-coed (along the A5 road).

OVERVIEW/INTEREST
Explores three of the highest and most dramatic peaks in Snowdonia.
Contrasting scenery of open moorland and expansive cliff faces.
Exquisite views of the Nant Ffrancon pass and Anglesey.

FOOTPATHS
Paths are very clear for most of walk, and early sections are waymarked.
Higher sections pass through areas of some exposure where care is needed. These may be treacherous in poor visibility.
Compass is essential.

GRADING   Difficult
TIME ALLOWANCE   6½ hours
DISTANCE
Excluding height   16.5km (10.3 miles)
TOTAL HEIGHT GAINED   1,237m (4,057ft)
PRINCIPAL HEIGHTS
Carnedd Dafydd 1,044m (3,426ft)
Carnedd Llewelyn 1,064m (3,492ft)
Yr Elen 962m (3,157ft)

The way to Carnedd Dafydd   *Allow 2½ hours*

Start this walk from the car park in Bethesda. Unfortunately, this car park is not shown explicitly on the map, but it is well sign-posted from the A5 in the centre of Bethesda and is free. At the time of writing it had recently been upgraded and enlarged. From the start of this route there are some rewarding views. The abundance of churches in Bethesda (there are 11 in 1sq km/¼sq mile!) provides a unique foreground to the Glyderau to the s and the Carneddau lying slightly to the E.

Leave the car park by the top (most E) exit and cross the waste ground so that you descend slightly to the wide gravel track that runs along the s edge. After about 50 paces a much narrower pathway leaves to the R and ascends the short bank between two buildings, heading to the w. Follow this and it will lead you to a tarmac road in a residential area of Bethesda, where you should turn R. Follow this road until it reaches a junction, where you turn sharp L and double back along another tarmac road. This section is very steep but short, since you leave by the next junction to the R. The subsequent section of the route is more straightforward and you should follow the long tarmac road as it weaves through the houses and cottages high above the centre of the village, heading SE. The road will cross a noisy river, the Afon Ffrydlas, which is hidden from view. Meanwhile, the w side of the Nant Ffrancon rises dramatically to the R. The road joins another from the R and you should continue up the slight incline, still walking SE.

This quiet road passes a small food store on the L, should you need any extra supplies. Beyond this, the route quickly winds up into the sparsely populated lower grassland of the Carneddau proper. There are numerous side roads and tracks leaving from both sides, which should be disregarded. After a few hundred paces the road passes over another boisterous river, the Afon Caseg, at a point where a few houses are located.

The road forks to the L up a steep hill, but this should be disregarded and you should follow the track to the SE. This road subsequently passes over another river, the Afon Llafar, via a substantial but narrow road bridge. There are pretty views both up- and downstream of the boiling river and waterfall in a small wood.

The road climbs out of the gully in which the river runs and heads off for the settlement of Tyddyn-du, to the SW. Before this, a track leaves to the L which you should follow. This track is marked 'Private' and various signs warn of danger. However, these officially refer to the grounds lying beyond a wide gate a few paces further on. Keeping to the R, climb over the fence on this side via an L-stile and continue to the L of a small stream, walking past a number of wizened trees that line the pretty meadow which follows. The path is clear and rocky, but you may need to stoop under the wind-twisted trees. At the top of the field you should cross a drystone wall via an L-stile that is partially hidden by trees to the L. From here the path turns sharp R to regain its prevailing bearing of ESE and enters an area of scrubland and marsh. The path is clear and wide with a confused array of boot-prints leading the way. The ground can be very wet, especially away from the path, and in winter the surface water can freeze to form large areas of slippery ground.

The route descends slightly before continuing up a gentle but constant gradient, passing over several L-stiles and through some derelict drystone farm buildings. The route is now waymarked regularly by distinctive black posts along the path. The way remains clear and, having drifted away from the Afon Cenllusg, now follows the course of the Afon Llafar which runs a few paces to the L, in a wide and shallow valley. After about 0.5km (⅓ mile) of steady climbing across the rough moorland you will reach an L-stile to the L of a wrought-iron gate. This marks the beginning of the open country that is synonymous with the Carneddau. The first un-interrupted views of the Carneddau range can be enjoyed from here; to the E you will be able to observe the peaked W slopes of Yr Elen leading to the summit of Carnedd Llewelyn, some 2km (1¼ miles) distant; to the SE the recommended route of

ascent – Mynydd Du – can be discerned, and the summit of Carnedd Dafydd lies beyond.

The ground is now comprised of stubbly grass interspersed with areas of marsh to either side of the path, which is clear and wide. In addition, there are more waymarkers which serve as valuable guides when this moorland is more challenging in misty weather. The path approaches the Afon Llafar, which leaves the Carneddau to the W. You should reach another L-stile, after which the path continues as before. Presently you will approach an old iron enclosure to your L, which is part of the disused dam workings that decorate the banks of the river at this stage. This serves as a distinct marker (MR 650653), where you should strike off the main path which leads to the foot of Carnedd Dafydd and begin your scent of Mynydd Du to the R.

The ascent of Mynydd Du is not easy, since the terrain continues as stubbly, uneven grass but now up a steeper gradient. As you continue to climb the grass begins to give way to areas of shale in places, especially around Foelgraig. The gradient is unrelenting for almost 2km (1¼ miles), as the distinctive spur develops into a substantial ridge. However, either side of this ridge spectacular views abound. The Carneddau stretch out ahead and to the L and, further afield, the peaks that comprise the W side of the Nant Ffrancon rise eerily on your R. As you gain height the characteristic triangular side view of Elidir Fawr can be seen rising to the SW, between Mynydd Perfedd and Foel Goch. This fine view will accompany much of the forth-coming route.

As you zigzag your way up the mountain, the ridge will quickly become precipitous to the E, with steep screes contrasting sharply with the bulbous grass of the W. After a few hundred paces the gradient relents, as you reach the plateau which forms part of Cwm Moch. Cwm Moch is crowned by a distinctive outcrop on the ridge and provides an attractive viewpoint and resting place prior to the final ascent. Some care is required here, since there are sheer slopes to the E which are about 100m (328ft) high. From this location the ascent continues due S and the path drifts away from the edge of the ridge to sweep up Foel Merich.

As the ascent continues the terrain becomes consistently more barren and rock strewn. The grass that is present is very short and you will become exposed to the harsh winds that howl up the Nant Ffrancon. The path steepens greatly and becomes a little more challenging because of the slate-ridden terrain. In fine weather you should be able to view the complete range of the Glyderau to the sw, including Tryfan, which is almost looked down upon from the lofty heights of Carnedd Dafydd at 1,044m (3,426ft). The summit is a moonscape and is marked by a large cairn and a couple of drystone shelters, which allow you to take in the impressive views: to the e Carnedd Llewelyn dominates the landscape, while to the n you can see Anglesey and the sea beyond. In contrast to the mountainous relief of n Snowdonia, Anglesey is a smooth, flat landscape, usually a blue-grey colour in fine weather.

A ghostly Yr Elen braves a winter storm.

The way to Carnedd Llewelyn *Allow 2 hours*

From the summit you should proceed due e. The path, which has kept away from the steep black cliffs of the n side of Carnedd Dafydd, now leads to within metres of their edge. There are numerous cairns to guide you in poor visibility and several paths climb on to the ridge from the n. Disregard these and continue along the ridge as it gradually turns to head ne. A refreshing view is possible to your r along Peny waun-wen towards Pen yr Helgi Du. At the foot of this is the small reservoir of Ffynnon Llugwy.

You should now be proceeding ne and in clear weather you will be able to look directly down the valley formed by Carnedd Dafydd and Carnedd Llewelyn to the n. There are few hills and mountains to interrupt this view towards Anglesey. Bethesda, with its abundance of churches, is a mere scattering of slate houses on this vast plateau stretching to the Menai Straits, and the flat

character of this coastal section of land contrasts sharply with the vast peaks of the Carneddau. The ridge path is clear and, providing you lose no height, the route is straightforward. In poor visibility frequent compass bearings – beginning ENE and gradually changing to NE – are essential, because it is easy to venture from the ridge path and lose your way. Be especially careful because of the treacherous cliffs to the N, and there are many sheep tracks that can confuse in the mist. However, the correct path is wide and clear and will turn slightly to the N as the incline increases rapidly for the final ascent of Carnedd Llewelyn. The flat, grassy ridge path now consists almost entirely of dust and rock and there is much loose slate, so be careful in winter conditions. The terrain is similar to the summit of Carnedd Dafydd. However, the summit of Carnedd Llewelyn, at 1,064m (3,492ft), is different in that it is a wide dome and is more isolated than its partner. Indeed, the breadth of the summit restricts the surrounding visibility to the immediate foreground and very distant horizons.

The summit of Carnedd Llewelyn affords rewarding views of the characteristic Black Ladders – the black cliffs on the N side of Carnedd Dafydd. If you look closely just below the summit, you will see distinctive rings in these cliffs which resemble the ramparts of a castle and are quite unique. These cliffs are black because they face NE and hence are very wet. In addition, the long ridge of Mynydd Du can be seen to the N of these.

The way to Yr Elen and back to Bethesda
Allow 2 hours

The descent route proceeds to the NW, following the ridge running parallel to Mynydd Du. This wide ridge leads to Yr Elen, an unusual peak that forms the highest part of a large cwm called Cwm Caseg. As you circumnavigate this you will descend sharply down a path of fine, loose slate which can become slippery and requires an ice-axe in winter. To you R you can see into the cwm and should spot a small lake, Ffynnon Caseg, at its base. The slate-ridden slope leads to a small saddle, which is covered with short grass and a scattering of rocks

and boulders. To your left the lower N peaks of the Nant Ffrancon escort you beyond Mynydd Du. These peaks are normally draped in a mysterious gry-blue haze from this distance and have easily recognizable, characteristic shapes.

After sweeping down the zigzag path to the saddle there is a short incline turning slightly to the N on to the rather rectangular peak of Yr Elen, at 962m (3,157ft). Since the summit is only 100m (110yd) wide, you will soon begin to descend once more and should follow the spur that leads to the NW, sweeping round to head eventually due W near to the outcrop of Foel Ganol. This is a most peculiar descent, since it resembles a fairground slide: three sweeping drops divided by two distinct crags and intermediate flat sections. You will lose height quickly but the uneven ground may make descending hard work, especially if your calf muscles are tired from previous ascents! As you approach the final stages of the descent, known as Braich y Brysgyll, you should bear gradually to the L, walking due W. You will soon reach the valley floor between the Carneddau. The view to the SW puts these giant cousins of the Glyderau in full perspective, as they now stand either side of you.

The valley floor is covered in long grass and reeds and can be quite marshy. Although the path becomes faint, you should find navigation is easy as you head due W towards the old dam workings, which from a distance can be mistaken for a footbridge. In poor visibility a compass bearing due W will lead you to the path that runs along the base of Mynydd Du (along Cwm Pen-llafar) which, on bearing R (NW), takes you to the iron enclosure which was encountered on the ascent.

From the dam workings, you need to cross the Afon Llafar. There are numerous possible places: follow the sheep! Walk up the short slope opposite, which leads to the path and the iron enclosure. From here, you should retrace your steps to Bethesda to the NW. You can follow the waymarkers across the russet countryside and down the gentle descent past the bubbling rivers and streams of the moor. You may be fortunate and view the sunset on the distant hills of Gwyn Wigau, Drosgl and Bera Bach to the NE.

Alternative routes

The north-western panorama of Bethesda and beyond.

ESCAPES

There are few escape routes to be recommended on this route, since the sheer faces of the Carneddau prevent any descents that are both quick and safe. If you are on the Mynydd Du section of the walk, it is best by far to retrace your steps. Otherwise, perseverance and frequent compass bearings are essential for a safe descent from Carnedd Llewelyn via Yr Elen. The w slopes of this mountain are reasonably gentle, but they are scattered with loose screes and consequently do not present a safe descent.

EXTENSIONS

This route forms a natural circuit and cannot be extended easily. The next most N peak of the Carneddau, Foel Grach at 976m (3,202ft), could be visited by strong walkers, and Garnedd Uchaf at 926m (3,038ft) might also be included. However, from these summits there are no suitable routes of descent to Bethesda other than returning to Carnedd Llewelyn and following the recommended route. It should be noted that as this walk is already quite challenging, these extensions will turn it into a real expedition!

Route 4: SNOWDON: THE WATKIN PATH

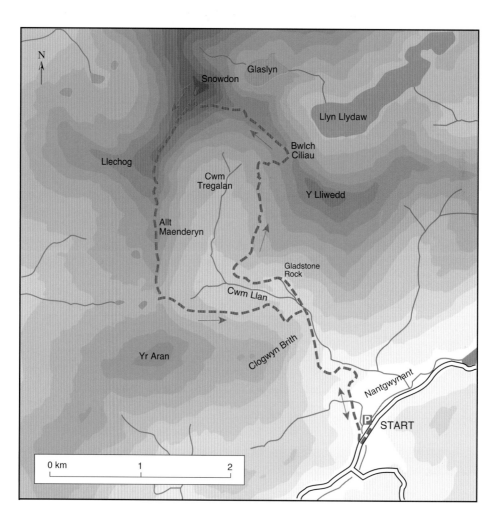

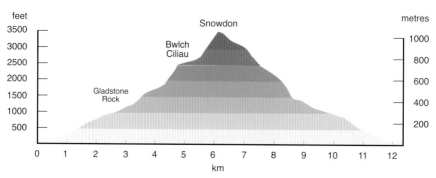

3

NORTHERN SNOWDONIA

Route 4 • Snowdon: the Watkin Path

The way to Bwlch Ciliau   *Allow 2 hours*

From the car park at Nantgwynant walk along the layby, SW in the direction of Beddgelert. You will pass some public toilets on your L and cross the Afon Glaslyn via a wide footbridge before joining the A498. This road connects Beddgelert with the A4086 to Capel Curig and can be busy, particularly in summer. Cross the road and head for the tarmac track to the N, with the small forest of Clogwyn Melyn on its L. This road is very flat since it runs across the floor of the Nantgwynant valley; it passes very close to the smooth waters of the Afon Glaslyn before striking off to the NW after a few hundred paces up a smaller, rockier path on the L. This path is sheltered by some established rhododendrons and mountain ash and climbs steadily. It is made of well-drained pebbles and gravel and is wide and defined, with a wire fence to the R. Beyond the fence pleasant views are possible up the Nantgwynant valley, looking NE.

After a few hundred more paces you will pass through a worn gate and, as the route turns gradually round to the W, the view of Clogwyn Brith, a large spur heading NE, will open up ahead. A deep scar divides Clogwyn Brith in the form of a disused incline from the past slate quarrying industry, which haunts the lower sections of this walk. Here you will also pass several small waterfalls to your R, as the path sweeps gradually uphill in a wide arc in front of Clogwyn Brith. The remains of the miners' cartway truncates this arc, but you should keep to the path. Just after you pass the waterfalls and the path winds around Clogwyn Brith, it splits. Part of it ventures NE across the river via a narrow footbridge. Disregard this path and continue due N as before.

Just past the incline you will pass through a rust-red K-gate and the path approaches the Afon Cwm Llan, which it will eventually cross via a low bridge. A path leaves to the SW: this forms part of the return route and should be disregarded for now. Ahead of you the large outcrops around the Gladstone Rock are visible in fine weather, with the summit of Snowdon presently hidden by the sweeping SE spur of Craig Ddu. Slightly to the W is the long ridge, peaked by Allt Maenderyn, which will be investigated shortly. This peak is the highest point of the massive southern spur of Snowdon and is a grassy ridge sprinkled with glacial debris.

The gradient reduces as you reach the lower sections of Cwm Llan, and you will pass some derelict quarry buildings to your R, together with several tall trees, before the path and river separate to avoid the large rocky outcrops ahead. Continue to the R of these, heading NW.

After a few hundred paces the path meanders slightly uphill across a wider section of grass, and you will pass the Gladstone Rock to the L. This is a small, smooth outcrop amid much larger rock formations, and is the place where Gladstone, the Prime Minister of the time, addressed the local people on 13 September 1892 and opened the Watkin Path, which is named after the railway magnate Sir Edward Watkin. There is a rather worn plaque on the side of the outcrop commemorating this event.

The path gradually changes course, heading due W for more rugged mine relics as it passes to the E end of Craig Ddu. The gradient increases and the terrain becomes more uneven and rugged. To the NE stands Y Lliwedd and straight ahead, to the N, the full aspect of Snowdon is visible if the weather is clear. From this viewpoint the mountain resembles a collossal, misshapen pile of slate and is quite daunting. It stands a further 700m (2,297ft) in height beyond. The huge cwm over which Snowdon stands is called Cwm Tregalan. This is flanked by Y Lliwedd to the E and Allt Maenderyn to the W, with the Snowdon summit in the centre. Cwm Tregalan presents an incredibly vast expanse and is one of the premier high-level valleys in Snowdonia.

The path now reaches a collection of immense slate tips and a long-derelict slateworks with many vacant window-frames. From these slate heaps of the valley floor the path heads N, through further shale tips and the remnants of mining machinery of the last century. The path steepens quickly and becomes the Watkin Path, as denoted on the map. This path is efficient, gaining height rapidly and crossing occasional small streams and tributaries. It is much looser than previously encountered and requires more thought and care. To the S the lonely outpost of Snowdon, Yr Aran, stands with its sheer face of Y Geuallt adding an eerie presence to the surroundings. There are several cairns along the path at this stage and it is well worn and clear. The steep gradient results in the path being well drained, uneven and very rocky. Further on, the vegetation is displaced by the morass of boulders and rocks that scatter the western slopes of Y Lliwedd. This section of the route continues for more than 1km (⅝ mile) due N, and the climb is quite relentless!

According to legend, Cwm Tregalan and the upper sections of Cwm Llan are the site of the last battle of King Arthur. It is said that the king's army gradually forced the Saxons further into the wintery cwm until, at nightfall, they reached the crest. Arthur is said to have been slain in this area, possibly by a volley of arrows. The NE face of Snowdon is called Bwlch-y-Saethau – Pass of the Arrows – and may be named after this event. The king's body was then carried to the shores of Llyn Llydaw by one of his loyal knights, where it was set afloat and disappeared into the mist aboard a black barge. The remaining knights sought shelter on Y Lliwedd.

At around the 600m (1,969ft) contour (MR 616536) the path turns sharply to the E. This turn is sharp enough to have caused the path to scatter over a relatively wide area in comparison with the lower slopes. The route zigzags to the E, searching for the easiest route on the now steep slopes. The final section leading to the top of the ridge, Bwlch Ciliau (744m/2,441ft), is on a NE bearing. This leaves you on the w side of the ridge, to the NW of Y Lliwedd and SE of Bwlch-y-Saethau. The spectacular peak of Y Lliwedd rises sharply and the full aspect of this arête can be appreciated from this position. If you venture carefully across the ridge to the NE side, another dramatic view appears before you: Llyn Llydaw stretches out to the NE, with the smaller lake of Glaslyn to the w. Beyond these stands the jagged edge of Crib Goch, leading to Garnedd Ugain in the w and completing this most spectacular view of the Snowdon Horseshoe. Looking ENE, beyond Llyn Llydaw, it is possible to view Llynau Mymbyr, while Carnedd Moel Siabod lies on the horizon due E.

The Snowdon massif from Llynnau Mymbyr.

The way to the Snowdon summit

Allow 2 hours

To continue, it is best to return to the NW side of the ridge, since this is less exposed. The summit is eventually scaled from the NW side, from Bwlch Main. The ridge walking is relatively easy for 0.5km (⅓ mile) as the path is well worn, clear and relatively free from rocks. The summit is still some 300m (984ft) higher and the massif rises dramatically in front of you to the NW. There is very little vegetation at this height on these SE slopes of Snowdon.

As you approach you will deviate slightly to the w and even lose a small amount of height. After a short distance the path becomes progressively more

exposed and steepens rapidly. You must concentrate on placing your feet safely, as the surface is very loose and there is a substantial drop to the s. There may be other walkers taking apparently more direct routes on a more N bearing, but you should not be tempted to follow because this is foolhardy: despite Snowdon's popularity, it remains a dangerous maintain and the risks entailed do not outweigh any saving in time – and there is certainly no saving in effort! You should stay on a bearing of due w, keeping to the worn path wherever possible.

The final steps of the climb deteriorate into a zigzag scramble for almost 100 paces, which leaves you on the summit ridge. From this viewpoint (MR 609542), a huge wall-like spur named Llechog slopes down gracefully in the w to the three lakes of the w slopes of Snowdon – Llyn Nadroedd, Llyn Coch and Llyn Glas – with the larger Llyn Ffynnon-y-gwas beyond them. To the N is the partner of Llechog, another huge spur named Clogwyn D'ur Arddu, which forms the N edge of the huge cwm of Cwm Clogwyn. Beyond this to the NW lies Moel Cynghorion, which is 674m (2,211ft) in height. In the distance, on a similar bearing, are the solitary peaks of Moel Eilio and Mynydd Mawr, the latter being slightly to the s. Due w, in fine weather the beautiful folded slopes of the Nantlle ridge are visible.

The Snowdon summit lies to the NE of your present position, a few hundred paces further on along quite a steep climb. Once again, the path is deteriorating with use and requires some care. Severe erosion has resulted in it sinking in places up to a metre below the level of the adjacent terrain. Within about 100 paces the Snowdon Mountain Railway summit station becomes visible. The summit is only a further few paces from here, although the gradient does not relent until the very top, so you will probably need a rest amid the swirling steam from the trains.

The summit of Snowdon is usually busy, unless you set off very early and preferably before the trains start. From Snowdon, many of the ranges in the region are visible. To the NE the Glyderau are the dominant feature on the horizon, beyond Garnedd Ugain and Crib Goch. To the SE is the now familiar Y Lliwedd, and to the s are the peaks surrounding Beddgelert including Cnicht, Moel Hebog and Y Arddu. The w vista contains the Nantlle Ridge and the peaks of Mynydd Tal-y-mignedd and Mynydd Drws-y-coed. You are also surrounded by an assortment of lakes; to the E lie Llyn Llydaw and Llyn Glaslyn and to the w Llyn Nadroedd, Llyn Coch and Llyn Glas.

The way to Allt Maenderyn and back to Nantgwynant
Allow 1½ hours

From the summit, retrace your steps s towards the distinctive curved spur of Llechog, until you arrive at the point where you reached the summit ridge from the Watkin Path (MR 609542). Do not follow the path of ascent, but instead continue sw along Bwlch Main. Once you have completed the brief steep descent from the summit the terrain changes from loose scree to short grass interspersed with boulders, rocks and sheep, and the gradient reduces considerably.

The path steepens again slightly as you follow the narrow ridge of Bwlch Main and after 0.5km (⅓ mile) another path leads off to the w. This descends via Llechog to the area of the Beddgelert forest and should be disregarded. Continue on due s. If the cloud is sufficiently high, the two peaks of Allt Maenderyn (704m/2,310ft) and Yr Aran (747m/2,451ft) should be visible ahead, with the larger Moel Hebog (782m/2,566ft) to the sw. The route is improved by cairns positioned along this section and, guided by these, you will be able to observe further views of the skeletal Crib Goch peeping over Bwlch Ciliau to the NE. Further on the terrain deteriorates somewhat into shale and loose slate, and you should cross a fence via an L-stile before following a gradual rise to reach the summit of Allt Maenderyn. From this summit, in fine weather a collection of small lakes is visible to the sw, and the Beddgelert forest stretches out beyond in a deep emerald carpet. You should also be able to see the old quarry settlements in the valley to the E, with their associated slate tips scattered on either side of the meandering river of the Afon Cwm Llan.

Snowdon and the spur of Craig Ddu from the disused cartway.

The route now descends positively and there is more grass underfoot as you reach a crossroads with three paths to choose from. One heads off s for the pointed peak of Y Aran, while another leads w to Beddgelert. Disregard these and follow the path to your L heading E, descending a lush, grassy slope towards the disused quarries. After only about 100 paces the correct route tracks SE instead of descending immediately to the valley floor. In the valley below there is a curious plot of upright slate pieces with sweethearts' names scratched on them, and a dismantled tramway staggered with short grass where the sleepers once lay.

The path keeps to the high ground, and because of this avoids much of the wetter land below. After about 1km (⅝ mile) it connects with the old tramway and thereby becomes much more defined. However, be vigilant for a smaller, steeper path leaving to the NE after about 200 paces, since this is the recommended route: the tramway eventually leads to the head of a disused incline (the 'scar' in Clogwyn Brith encountered earlier) which is very dangerous and the descent of which should not be attempted. The correct path leaves to the R of a large tributary immediately after fording it (MR 619519) via a considerable embankment, and descends gradually towards the Afon Cwm Llan below. This path, some 200 paces long, is waymarked by posts and large stones, presumably taken from the tramway. You will join the original path of ascent just beyond the wide footbridge that crosses the river and a few hundred paces before the waterfalls encountered previously. From here, retrace your steps past the spidery waterfalls, around the sweeping cwm and along the path, which quickly becomes sheltered in the young trees on either side. This leads down to Nantgwynant for some well-earned refreshment!

Alternative routes

ESCAPES

This route is a relatively short and economic ascent of Snowdon and cannot be shortened safely, other than by retracing your steps prior to reaching the summit ridge.

EXTENSIONS

This route can be extended by including the peak of Y Lliwedd. To do this, turn R at Bwlch Ciliau (MR 619537) heading SE, and climb the steep, rocky path to the summit 0.5km (⅓ mile) away. After this, retrace your steps NW to continue on the recommended route to the Snowdon summit.

Further along the route, it is possible to include Y Aran by heading due N, exercising care and respect for the sheer sides and loose screes that make up this mountain. Once again, you will need to return to the original route and descend as recommended. This can be done most effectively by descending the long E ridge of Yr Aran for several hundred paces. Then you should follow the path down to the embankment at MR 619519 to join the recommended route.

The combination of both these extensions necessitates prolonged, steep walking and should be only attempted by the super-fit!

Route 5: TRYFAN AND THE GLYDERAU

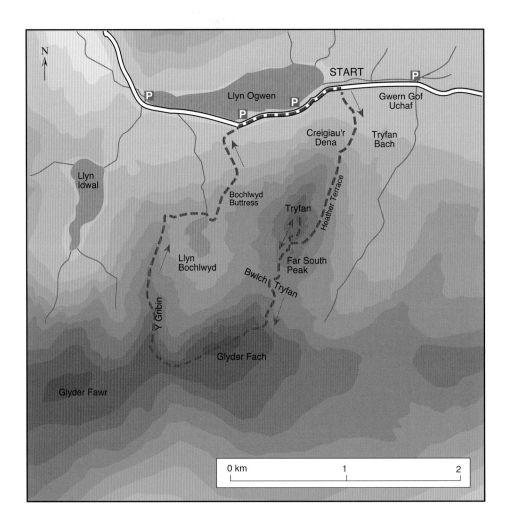

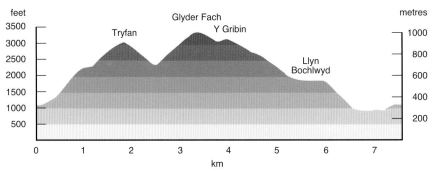

Route 5 • Tryfan and the Glyderau

STARTING LOCATION

E of Llyn Ogwen on wide verges along the A5 road.

OLM 17/MR 667605.

Public toilets at w end of Llyn Ogwen.

ALTERNATIVE STARTING LOCATION

None.

PUBLIC TRANSPORT

Bus route Bangor–Capel Curig (along the A5 (T) road).

OVERVIEW/INTEREST

Spectacular ascent, via Heather Terrace, of the peaks at the head of the Nant Ffrancon.

Exquisite views of all Snowdonia, including Bristly Ridge, Glyder Fach and Tryfan itself.

Features include the Adam and Eve Stones, The Cantilever and other unusual outcrops, and the Castle in the Winds.

Exhilarating descent via Y Gribin, passing by Llyn Bochlwyd.

FOOTPATHS

Paths can be unclear in steep sections and treacherous in winter, when crampons and ice-axe are essential.

Very exposed in several places.

Large boulder terrain requires care.

Compass is essential.

GRADING   Difficult

TIME ALLOWANCE   6 hours

DISTANCE

Excluding height   9km (5.6 miles)

TOTAL HEIGHT GAINED   1,189m (3,825ft)

PRINCIPAL HEIGHTS

Tryfan 915m (3,003ft)

Far South Peak 830m (2,724ft)

Glyder Fach 994m (3,262ft)

The way to Heather Terrace and Tryfan

Allow 2½ hours

Tryfan is one of the most famous mountains in Wales and possibly Great Britain. It is made up of a narrow arête that shoots up from the roadside very rapidly and is crowned by three peaks. These lie within a few hundred metres of each other, with the main one denoted by two large boulders known as the Adam and Eve Stones. The very characteristic shape of Tryfan is easily distinguished from its many outlying neighbours and serves as a useful landmark. From the main body of Tryfan, the s ridge sweeps down to a short saddle before climbing vigorously again, via the notorious Bristly Ridge, towards Glyder Fach and the s end of the Nant Ffrancon. For the walker in search of exhilaration and almost alpine mountain terrain, Tryfan and the Glyderau should not be missed!

The popularity of Tryfan is evident by the substantial parking available nearby: you can park at the w end of Llyn Ogwen or in one of the vast laybys along the banks of the lake. At the E end of the lake, where the A5(T) heads off E and straight, there are long, wide verges along the road that can also be used and these are most suitable for the proposed route. It is best to avoid weekends and bank holidays, since after 10am parking can be difficult and there might not be room on the summit! Despite its popularity, Tryfan poses severe hazards to those who are ill-equipped, especially in winter: be sure to check your equipment and provisions before you set off.

Start from the layby a few hundred metres from the E end of Llyn Ogwen at the L-stile (MR 667605) opposite Glan Dena. This stile is to the L of a wooden gate and is immediately followed by another L-stile that crosses a wire fence to the R. Cross this stile and leave the fencing and its accompanying path for the steeper ground to the SE. The path heads off SE, effectively climbing around the N lower slopes of Tryfan, and you should not descend into the wide valley to your L. This area is marked by Tryfan Bach (Little Tryfan), a large, sheer slab of rock to the E that is popular with climbers. The recommended route continues parallel to this, climbing steadily over grass and rock terrain. The path loses some definition in places, but navigation should not be difficult. The gradient remains constant for several hundred metres.

To the E you should be able to see the farm buildings at Gwern Gof Uchaf, usually distinctive due to the brightly coloured tents on the campsite nearby. To the W the impressive mountain of Y Garn can be seen, while to the NW is the immense mass of Pen yr Ole Wen. On a clear day, looking NE the smoother peaks of Y Braich and Pen Llithrig y Wrach can be observed sweeping down from the Carneddau in the N.

The terrain develops gradually into grass and boulders with ferns in between. In the autumn the ferns turn a vivid orange that remains until early spring. As you continue the ground becomes wetter and you are now a considerable height above the road. The Nant Ffrancon is popular with the RAF for low-altitude flying and you may be surprised by a supersonic aircraft sweeping around Ogwen, almost level or possibly even below you! The path steepens and you begin to approach the large crags of Tryfan proper above you.

When you are level with Tryfan Bach, you will reach a crossroads of paths: the route that heads up from Gwern Gof Uchaf and Tryfan Bach crosses your present track. You should turn R to head due W. The path is now clearer and heads for a large fissure in the mountain ahead. The gradient increases considerably and you may need to use your hands to steady yourself. The wide gully between outcrops heads up to the E of Creigiau'r Dena. The path continues its uneven route, now heading SW and crossing small scrambles and coarse screes, until you are near to the upper sections of Tryfan. These resemble a large tower of rock above you. The path now loses some definition, so be vigilant, and crosses steep sections of large boulders which can be tricky for the less experienced. After about 100 paces of steep, rocky

terrain the path flattens suddenly and the grass and heather return to the wide ledge that stretches out to the SSW. This lies midway up Tryfan and is known as Heather Terrace.

There are many routes of ascent on Tryfan, but not all can be classed as walks suitable for all abilities. Indeed, Tryfan is reputed to be impossible to climb without the use of your hands, since all routes entail some degree of scrambling. The

Icicles cling to the upper reaches of Heather Terrace.

ascents via the N ridge and anything attempting the w face can easily turn into full-blown graded scrambles and are therefore not recommended here. However, Heather Terrace is a valuable feature since it provides an easier route of ascent which entails less scrambling. It proceeds for just over 0.5km (⅓ mile) on a steady but relaxed incline. The terrace is wide and the path is clear. Pleasant views are afforded of Cwm Tryfan to the E and of the lesser peaks, such as Y Foel Goch, heading towards Capel Curig. While on Heather Terrace you should not be tempted by apparently easy gullies heading up to the R. There are several of these and, in general, they quickly transcend into difficult scrambles and virtual climbs that can be very dangerous. In winter, although Heather Terrace remains straightforward these gullies are transformed into sheets of ice that are best left to the experts!

The terrace passes beneath the peak and begins to widen considerably as it turns to face due w, and approaches the Far South Peak of Tryfan. The path crosses a drystone wall via an L-stile and you are left on the wide lower slopes, a few hundred paces s of the summit. You should turn R to head NNE, and follow the path as it winds steadily up the final few metres to the summit. However, do not become complacent. As the path continues, the wide ridge narrows rapidly and both sides steepen greatly. This is especially true to the R (E) where tall slabs, apparently stood on end, form a vertical wall about 30m (98ft) high. It is important to make everyone in your party aware of the dangers here, since the terrain is exposed and hazardous only a short distance from the path.

The path climbs steeply and the terrain changes to loose scree, gravel and large boulders. Soon the area widens slightly and you approach the two significant square boulders of the Adam and Eve Stones that mark the summit of Tryfan. There is a tradition that walkers feel compelled to step across the Adam and Eve Stones when reaching the top of Tryfan, and certainly the views from them are magnificent. News of the popularity of Tryfan has spread to the extent that there are usually numerous seagulls on the top in search of scraps from walkers' lunches!

It is not just the exhilaration of the climb that makes Tryfan popular, but also the tremendous views from the summit. Being a steep-sided peak, the views are not hindered by any foreground and you have an almost complete panorama. To the w lies the impressive peak of Y Garn with its lesser neighbours of Foel Goch and Mynydd Perfedd forming the w side of the immense Nant Ffrancon valley. Just behind these is Elidir Fawr. Further away, looking sw, is the Snowdon Horseshoe with Y Lliwedd, the Snowdon summit and Garnedd Ugain appearing most prominent. To the NW is Pen yr Ole Wen with the vast slopes of the Carneddau lying beyond, sometimes speckled with patches of snow. Nearer to Tryfan, to the sw, are the two huge, flat-topped peaks of Glyder Fach (nearest) and Glyder Fawr (further away and more to the w). These peaks are connected to Tryfan via the low saddle of Bwlch Tryfan and the renowned Bristly Ridge.

The way to Glyder Fach   *Allow 1½ hours*

From the summit of Tryfan head ssw, retracing your steps to the Far South Peak. This time you should disregard the L-stile that leads to Heather Terrace and continue ssw. The path descends rapidly to the R of the main arête and zigzags down towards the low saddle of Bwlch Tryfan that lies far below. You need to lose a great deal of height, while ahead of you the NE edge of Glyder Fach grows in perspective. This view comprises Bristly Ridge, which is a jagged edge of sharp, upright slabs with a pronounced gully ascending between them, and to the L of this a smoother slope, distinctive in summer as a wide, worn path while in winter the snow turns it into a white streak on the mountainside. You might be able to pick out fellow walkers trudging their way up. Bristly Ridge is exciting but treacherous and should only be attempted by those with adequate climbing skills. The recommended route follows the smoother, safer alternative.

You will quickly reach the saddle and pass a path that descends to the NW, towards the lake of Cwm Bochlwyd and Ogwen. This should be disregarded unless it is being used as an escape route. The recommended route runs over flat but stubbly ground towards a drystone wall and two L-stiles: Bristly Ridge heads off to the R beyond a loose mass of rock and disregards the stiles. Cross the wall via the stiles and follow the path carefully as it traverses the smooth slope to the E of the main ridge heading SSW once more. The gradient increases rapidly and the path widens, becoming loose and dusty. In winter it is often covered in hard snow and ice, necessitating the use of crampons and ice-axe. The slope continues for several hundred metres and eventually leaves you just beyond the top of Bristly Ridge on the wide, flat plateau before Glyder Fach (MR 658585).

The inclined scree and dust of the ascent from Bwlch Tryfan contrasts strongly with the open scrubland of Glyder Fach. This is strewn with rock chips and larger boulders and is very windswept. Consequently the path deteriorates, but navigation should not be difficult: keep a straight course heading SW. Both Glyder Fach and its higher neighbour, Glyder Fawr, have unusual summits that are marked by huge piles of large boulders and rock slabs. These are presumably the remnants of moraine deposited when glaciers left the area and do not lie flat but stand around in an array of positions. Indeed, Glyder Fawr has a spiky summit which can be seen on the horizon to the SW. Glyder Fach is more characteristic, since the rocks have formed The Cantilever: a seemingly precariously placed slab of rock resembling a diving board. It is actually quite safe and fellow walkers are often seen standing on the end of it, apparently in mid-air.

The summit of Glyder Fach is found at the top of a pile of large boulders. This position is particularly good for views along the Nant Ffrancon, provided the sun has not yet left it. You can also get a view of the Snowdon Horseshoe to the SW, although the spiky-topped Glyder Fawr obscures part of this. On fine, clear days, as are often found in early spring, the view can be extensive. Looking S and SW it is possible to see many peaks including Carnedd Moel Siabod, the Moelwynion, the Rhinogyll and sometimes even the long massif of Cadair Idris. These giants are complemented by the view of the beaches around Porthmadog.

The way to Y Gribin and back to Ogwen
Allow 2 hours

From Glyder Fach you should continue SW: the plateau resumes quickly after the summit boulders and the walking is easy for a few hundred paces. The plateau ends at another famous Snowdonia landmark: Castell y Gwynt, the Castle in the Winds (MR 655582). This is a large outcrop of slim shafts of rock pointing skywards that to the more imaginative might resemble some diabolical castle! It indicates the transition from the summit plateau to the narrow saddle of Bwlch y Ddwy-Glyder and you need to climb over it. As you approach Castell y Gwynt this appears daunting, since it is the size of a large building and is spectacular. As its colloquial name indicates, the wind is prone to howl up the Nant Ffrancon and through this gap, adding greatly to its allure. However, the path is clear and with the minimum of effort it is possible to clamber up through the middle of the outcrop and back on to the path again. It is worth noting that Castell y Gwynt is most impressive from the N, so take your time to appreciate the view.

The path proceeds for a few hundred metres further, gradually changing to head due W at the lowest point of the saddle and then migrating further to the N. The path sticks rigidly to the edge of Cwm Bochlwyd and you should be able to see the lake of Llyn Bochlwyd far below you. If the mist is restricting visibility you should follow the path carefully and study your compass, since there are steep drops to both N and S.

As you follow the edge of Cwm Bochlwyd round, the gradient begins to increase and the path can clearly be seen to follow the edge of a small inclined plateau to the S; another path heads off just S of due W for Glyder Fawr and this should be disregarded (MR 651583). The climb is easy and the terrain grassy for a short distance. After this, the ridge of Y Gribin begins to form rapidly, with Cwm Bochlwyd and Cwm Cneifion (the Nameless Cwm) sweeping in on either side to render it only a few metres wide. You should be heading due N as the grass disappears quickly to be replaced by rocks and scree. For a while the path follows the top of the undulating ridge, but once the ridge begins to descend it falls slightly to the L (W) of the ridge where there is less exposure. Take great care on this descent, since the apparently benign upper rocky sections are followed by steep screes that run to the base of the Nameless Cwm: a walker's stick is always useful, while in winter the path can turn into a slippery, treacherous place, making an ice-axe essential.

Y Gribin is a long ridge and it does not give up its rugged character until the lower slopes. Suddenly the narrow edge widens into a boulder field and this is quickly followed by grass and a flatter area. Llyn Bochlwyd follows in parallel to the R. You should follow the ridge N until you reach a crossroads of paths where you turn R to head E: unfortunately, there are many paths in the area and the crossroads is not obvious, but the E path leaves when you are parallel with the N end of the lake. This path trundles over the lumpy lowland terrain and affords truly fantastic views of the W face of Tryfan for a considerable time. Also, looking S is the Glyder Fach massif that is hidden from sight further down the valley. This is an impressive granite arête, not unlike Tryfan.

You may find that the path you have followed E does not meet the lake as the map shows, but rather meets the river Nant Bochlwyd further N. This does not matter too much and you should cross the river where suitable and continue NE. The recommended route fords the river close to the lake and then turns to the N after a few paces. It then runs over Bochlwyd Buttress and heads for Llyn Ogwen. The terrain of grass and rocks makes walking easy and the path is clear, if a little boggy in places. Glyder Fach soon disappears from view to the rear because of intervening high ground, but Tryfan accompanies you all the way down.

A few hundred paces from the A5(T) road the ground steepens suddenly and falls away in front of you. The path changes course to head just N of due E, although this should be obvious as you are heading for the large layby visible on the R side of the road. The path winds its way down the bank to a large, red, circular K-gate. Pass through this into the layby. From this position (MR 659602), walk along the road back to your car. Take care on the road since it is very busy with heavy traffic.

Alternative routes

ESCAPES

Tryfan and the Glyderau can be transformed into hostile, dangerous places, especially in winter or if the mist comes in. The latter can happen very quickly, as banks of cloud roll up the Nant Ffrancon from the coast. Hence, an escape route is valuable if you should decide to return prematurely. Prior to Heather Terrace, it is best to simply retrace your steps via Tryfan Bach. Once you have reached the terrace or further, it is safest to continue and descend via Bwlch Tryfan, heading NW for Llyn Bochlwyd and picking up the recommended route later at MR 656594. Otherwise, it is best to follow the complete recommended route, remaining vigilant and relying on your compass.

EXTENSIONS

One of the great virtues of the Nant Ffrancon is its versatility, and this is particularly true of the upper regions around Tryfan. A worthwhile extension is to disregard the descent via Y Gribin and keep to the ridge (following to the W at MR 651582), which proceeds over easy terrain for Glyder Fawr. From the craggy summit of Glyder Fawr you can either return (heading just N of due E) and descend via Y Gribin, or follow the descent that heads off NW a few hundred paces from the summit. Great care is required here since, although the path is an eroded dusty swathe in summer, it is transformed in winter as it picks its way nimbly through the screes of Esgair Felen, which require respect. This area is also rather featureless and is daunting should visibility deteriorate. You should head for Llyn y Cwn for much of the descent, but the path will deviate from this course at the lower parts of the slope. Do not head any further N than is necessary, since there are the treacherous cliffs of the N face of Glyder Fawr and Twll Du (the Devil's Kitchen) to be aware of. From Llyn y Cwn it is possible to descend via Twll Du. A clear path for this heads NE from the lake; however, this is another descent that is complicated by snowfalls and ice-sheets in winter and care must be taken.

The real enthusiast can head NW from Llyn y Cwn and follow the long grassy ascent of Y Garn.

This lasts for 1km (⅝ mile) and really makes your calves burn at the end of this difficult route. From Y Garn you can follow the descent that leaves the edge of Cwm Clyd at MR 631597 (marked by a large cairn) and follows the smooth spur s of Pinnacle Crag to the N of Llyn Idwal and back to Ogwen.

Bear in mind that none of these extensions should be undertaken lightly and they are best attempted in summer, when there is plenty of daylight and particular sections are not complicated by snow and ice. The descents via Twll Du or Pinnacle Crag leave you at the W end of Llyn Ogwen, which will entail a considerable excursion along the road to complete the route.

Llyn Bochlwyd and the Nant Ffrancon from Tryfan's Far South Peak.

Route 6: MOEL EILIO, FOEL GRON AND FOEL GOCH

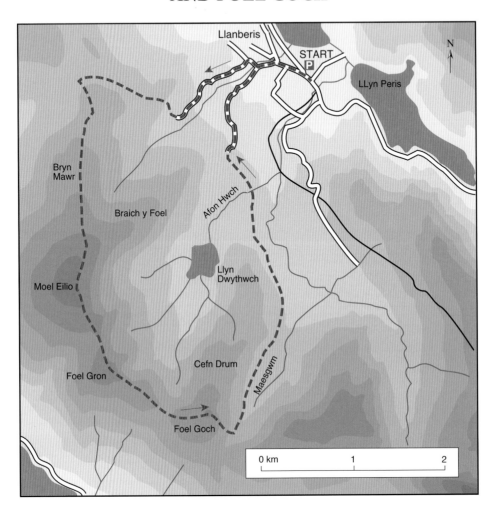

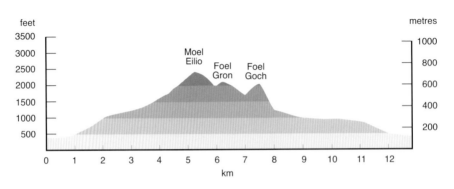

Route 6 • Moel Eilio, Foel Gron and Foel Goch

The way to Moel Eilio   *Allow 2½ hours*

The area immediately sw of Llanberis is dominated by a beautiful arch-shaped ridge which has dark crags on the E side that descend into small screes at their base. The highest point of this ridge is called Moel Eilio and is at the most N end, to the w of the long spur of Braich y Foel, which stretches out towards Llanberis in the E. The gentle arch of Moel Eilio is echoed by the two further summits along the ridge: those of Foel Gron and Foel Goch. At the base of these peaks, to the NE, is a sizeable lake called Llyn Dwythwch. This collects the drainage from the E slopes, which eventually reaches the larger lakes of Llyn Padarn and Llyn Peris at the valley floor. These dominate the NW end of the Llanberis Pass. The contrast of the flowing hillsides in the vicinity of Moel Eilio with the more popular, craggy mountains of the sw region of the Llanberis Pass presents a refreshing area for exploration, while also providing superb vantage points for viewing the surrounding larger mountains.

From the car park at Llanberis you need to turn L on to the footpath on the L side of the A4086. You should immediately notice a large craft centre on the R side of the road and an impressive mountain view ahead, a fair distance away. This view is of the Pen-y-pass region of the Llanberis Pass and is a combination of the foothills of the Glyderau (on the L) and the Snowdon horseshoe (on the R). A few paces further along the road you will pass the Dinorwig Museum on your L. This centre is dedicated to the building of a pumped-storage hydroelectric power station deep inside Elidir Fawr on the far side of Llyn Peris. It is well worth a visit and is very educational for children and adults alike.

About 200 paces further on there is a signpost denoting the village centre, to the R along a sharp fork on the R side of the road. Follow this and after a few paces you will pass a large church with a tower on the L; there are also several hotels which

Lush grassland at the base of Moel Eilio.

are of various sizes, such as the Dolafon Hotel on the L and the Gwynedd Hotel on the R. Subsequently there is a small garage and a small foodstore, should you need further supplies, which is open from 7am to 10.30pm on most days. You should now look out for a smaller tarmac road leaving to the L only a few paces beyond the foodstore. The correct turning is signposted for the youth hostel and the road is the Capel Coch Road. The tarmac immediately begins to climb away from Llanberis and there are a few residential houses on both sides. You will pass a small library on the R and a few paces further on a huge church to the L without a tower or spire. This building stretches along the road for a considerable distance; to the R a narrower tarmac road leaves up a short, steep hill and you should follow this.

This smooth tarmac road crosses the Afon Goch just to the R of a tall cottage and flattens slightly as it enters a more secluded residential area of modern cottages and similar white houses. After a few paces the road bends sharply to the L, while a smaller track continues ahead. Follow the road to the L, where you will find that it narrows and

deteriorates to the point where a thin stretch of grass develops down its middle. The road continues to climb steadily and views to the SE of the Llanberis Pass improve. A waymark footpath leaves to the L, which should be disregarded. As you continue along this quiet track into the hills, a small bank develops to the L hosting a variety of vegetation. This includes rowan and crab apple trees, brambles, ferns and ragwort. The track steepens and you will soon approach a wrought-iron gate across it bearing the sign 'Please shut'. Further on, there is a tidy footpath to the L which leads to some buildings at Cae'r-frân. Once again, you should disregard this and keep to the main track and the relentless climb. Further on you will pass a small, lone hawthorn on the L side of the road and several laybys. After a further 100 paces or so the drystone wall to the L becomes broken down and views abound of the S aspect. There is a foreground of emerald-coloured meadows and small fields with sheep dotted around. In the distance the patchwork farmland gives way to the vast N spurs of Foel Goch and Moel Cynghorion, while the Snowdon Mountain Railway might be seen ascending to the E of these. Continue along the track and you will notice a derelict building a short distance away on the L. Ahead of this the smooth spur of Braich y Foel, which forms the NE extent of Moel Eilio, comes into view to the S. The characteristic arch-shape of Moel Eilio is presently hidden behind this spur. Another path leaves to the L a few paces further on, but should be ignored in favour of the main track. The tarmac of this track has turned to gravel in most parts, but the track remains very clear.

After a further 200 paces or so, the track changes character near to a derelict farmstead on the roadside. Here (MR 567595) it turns sharp R and becomes uneven and ragged. The track traverses the top of an area of thick gorse to the R which slopes away towards Llanberis. The climb continues, turning from its heading of almost due N to that of WNW. With this change of direction the terrain to the R of the track changes too, from the familiar gorse to more austere grey slate tips. There is a large area of disused mines and waste heaps to the W of Llanberis and this path follows the S perimeter of this. At this stage views of more distant perspectives are obscured by the rising land all around. The track of gravel and grass flattens gradually and you should continue WNW, disregarding any paths leaving to the N over the drystone wall. To the S of you is the N tip of Bryn Mawr, the wide N slope of Moel Eilio. Although there are a couple of indistinct paths that leave to the L to ascend Bryn Mawr, it is recommended that you continue along the main track until you reach a gate with an L-stile. This is because the path is easier to follow from this point (MR 557599), and there is also a view of Mynydd Mawr on the horizon looking SSW. Beyond the gate the track continues among the mining industry relics. Disregard this and turn L to head SSE.

The beginning of the ascent of Bryn Mawr takes you across a confused array of furrowed paths up the grassy slope. These quickly recede and one clear path continues due S after a few hundred paces. The summit of Moel Eilio lies approximately 2km (1¼ miles) S from your present position. The gradient reduces after about 500 paces and the sweeping ridge comes into view ahead, looking very long indeed! However, the terrain is good, since the gradient remains constant until the last

few hundred paces to the summit and Bryn Mawr is a wide, grassy ridge with a clear path. This provides the opportunity for good views of Elidir Fawr to the E as you progress. The final few hundred paces to the summit of Moel Eilio scatter across a rather eroded section of loose rocks and shale in among the grass. The gradient increases considerably in the region where Braich y Foel joins from the E and continues until the summit, the climb becoming gruelling and long as it slips slightly to the E of the higher section of the ridge to the R. In mist, be sure to keep rigidly to the path – there are crags and steep screes to the E with featureless, grassy slopes to the W, so keep hold of youngsters. Just when the climb appears to be never-ending an L-stile over a fence comes into view. Beyond this, the summit cairn can be seen a few paces ahead.

The summit of Moel Eilio is a wide, flat, symmetrical plain with very short, weathered grass surrounding the wide cairn. There are good views of many mountains, including the W sides of Y Garn and Glyder Fawr. To the SE the view is dominated by Snowdon and the peak prior to it, Garnedd Ugain. The summit of Moel Eilio is pleasant and worth a long break or lunch stop in fine weather.

The way to Foel Gron and Foel Goch

Allow 2 hours

From the summit of Moel Eilio proceed SE, following to the R of a fence which runs along the summit ridge. Ahead you will be able to see the ridge stretching out in front towards the peaks of Foel Gron and Foel Goch. You will cross a corner made by the intersection of a fence and a drystone wall, via an L-stile. At this stage you should be able to see the lake of Llyn Dwythwch, far below in the bottom of the broad cwm of Cwm Dwythwch, to the E. To the S an unusual perspective of the Nantlle Ridge and the larger triangular mass of Mynydd Mawr is possible. To the E of these are the Snowdon lakes, Llyn y Gader and Llyny Dwarchen.

The descent develops into an easy walk across short grass and the occasional eroded area. The ridge is usually dry, since there are few hollows and ditches allowing water to collect. As you progress the path follows reasonably close to the edge of the ridge, providing superb views. Tryfan can be seen peeping between the mountains of the foreground in the E. The closest of these are the graceful slopes of Moel Cynghorion, about 3km (2 miles) distant. The large lake of Llyn Cwellyn is also visible in the valley of Nant y Betws to the s.

Beyond the slight peninsula near Bwlch Gwyn, the path starts to climb once again and approaches the edge of the ridge rapidly. The cliffs above Cwm Cesig are steep and sheer, providing an exhilarating part of the walk without affecting the comfortable terrain underfoot. The path loses some definition at this stage, but this should not cause any problem as you simply stay close to the edge of the ridge for the subsequent 1km (⅝ mile) at least. You will reach an unnamed summit which, at 629m (2,064ft), is actually higher than Foel Gron. Following this the path remains close to the cliff-tops for another 500 paces or so, during which there is a gradual descent and a slight change of direction from SE to due S, before a short incline to the summit of Foel Gron at 593m (1,946ft), MR 564566. You will encounter some rusty, disused gateposts between the unnamed peak and Foel Gron. Foel Gron marks the demise of the cliffs, and gradually the grassy slopes – which were encountered earlier on the N spur of Moel Eilio – begin to take over once more. Behind you (to the NW) the unnamed peak of Moel Eilio appear very similar to each other, their smooth-sloped forms quite unique for this area of Wales. Ahead of you, looking E, a large, lumpy spur by the name of Cefn Drum appears due N from the next peak of the walk, that of Foel Goch.

From Foel Gron there is another easy, grassy descent typical of the relaxed walking possible in the region of Moel Eilio. Ahead the summit of Snowdon is in view, with the distinctive neighbouring peak of Yr Aran. The descent quickly ends at another small

The gentle descent from Moel Eilio to Foel Gron, with Snowdon beyond.

saddle which immediately leads to Foel Goch. The climb is steep and, because it is the third such ascent of the route, can be quite strenuous. The path is clear and the climb lasts for a few hundred paces before the gradient reduces and the wide planar summit of Foel Goch is reached.

The summit of Foel Goch is similar to that of Moel Eilio in that it is wide and flat. Looking to the SE, excellent views of Moel Cynghorion are possible across the diverging valley of Maesgwm. Beyond this is the long, craggy spur of Clogwyn Du'r Arddu, which heads ESE towards Garnedd Ugain in the Snowdon Horseshoe. Looking to the N, the foreground comprises the lumpy spur of Cefn Drum leading to the village of Llanberis.

The way along Maesgwm back to Llanberis

Allow 1½ hours

The descent from Foel Goch is quite steep and follows an L-stile that crosses a fence on the summit. You should take some care here and not rush in case you slip. Be sure to keep to the SE bearing, as there are a few crags to the E of Foel Goch that will complicate your descent if you do not head far enough S.

The steepness of the descent ensures that it is over quickly and you will soon reach a wide path of loose slate heading NNE. Follow this along its straight course, heading down the secluded valley of Maesgwm for about 1km (⅝ mile). The path follows a route high above the river to the R and passes through a drystone wall, which then continues to the R. You will pass a rusty gate and an L-stile over a fence before some derelict buildings on the L surrounded by hawthorn trees. From this position the Snowdon Mountain Railway can be seen and the trains heard in the spring and summer seasons.

The path follows the E side of Cefn Drum as it turns gradually NNW. Deciduous trees line the path on the R and you will pass a house on the L. The spur of Cefn Drum undulates irregularly as it descends towards Llanberis, and after another 1km (⅝ mile) you will reach a gate and L-stile that lead to a bridge over the Afon Hwch. This is the main outflowing river from Llyn Dwythwch, which was viewed from the summit of Moel Eilio. At this stage (MR 575587) the path becomes a more defined road and heads NW. After a few hundred paces you will reach a gate secured by a rope and a further few hundred paces beyond will come to another gate prior to a small junction. This fork in the track is near a farm to the R at MR 573591. Disregard the L fork and take the tarmac road to the R. This road winds gently down the final few hundred paces to Llanberis. It is crossed by several gates and a few minor paths leave from either side, which should be ignored in favour of the tarmac. The road eventually passes close to the youth hostel, followed by a gradual increase in residential buildings and cottages. It soon reaches the junction near to the large church encountered early in the walk. From this position you should continue downhill into Llanberis for some well-earned refreshment at one of the many cafés or hotels.

Alternative routes

ESCAPES

The E side of the ridge crowned by Moel Eilio is impassable and therefore there are no recommended short cuts from the ridge. However, if you wish to omit Foel Goch due to fatigue, it is possible to traverse the higher reaches of Cefn Drum from the saddle at MR 566564. Following a contour faithfully (possibly by a sheep track) will lead you on to the rough plateau at a height of about 500m (1,641ft) along Cefn Drum. From here you should continue to traverse NE, heading downhill over the grassy W slopes of Maesgwm. This descent is not as steep as that of the SE side of Foel Goch, but it is a bit uneven and tiring on the legs. On this bearing you will reach the path along Maesgwm around the area where the drystone wall joins the path and near the hawthorn-covered derelict buildings. From here, follow the recommended main route back to Llanberis.

EXTENSIONS

This walk is self-contained and no extensions are recommended.

Route 7: FOEL-GOCH AND Y GARN FROM NANT PERIS

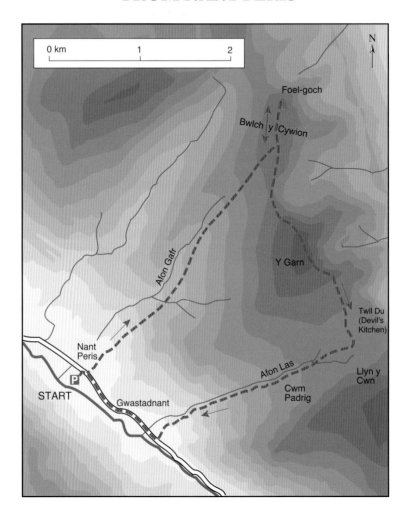

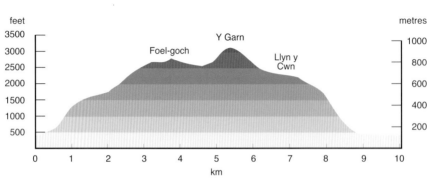

4

WESTERN SNOWDONIA AND THE LLEYN PENINSULA

Route 7 • Foel-goch and Y Garn from Nant Peris

STARTING LOCATION
Car park at Nant Peris.
OLM 17/MR 607583.
Capacity for 80 cars.
Public toilets (closed in winter) and picnic facilites.

ALTERNATIVE STARTING LOCATION
Nant Peris MR 605584 (no parking).

PUBLIC TRANSPORT
Bus route Carnarfon–Capel Curig (along A4086).

OVERVIEW/INTEREST
Expansive views of the S side of the Llanberis Pass,
   Elidir Fawr and Glyderau.
Pleasant descent via Cwm Padrig.

FOOTPATHS
Paths are clear in places but a compass is essential.
Extreme care is required, since the E faces of the
   Nant Ffrancon are sheer, especially in snow.
Middle sections are usually wet, and exposed
   moorland requires windproof clothing.

GRADING   Moderate
TIME ALLOWANCE   5½ hours
DISTANCE
Excluding height   11km (6.8miles)
TOTAL HEIGHT GAINED   1,028m (3,392ft)
PRINCIPAL HEIGHTS
Foel-goch 831m (2,727ft)
Y Garn 947m (3,108ft)

The way to Foel-goch
Allow 2½ hours

This walk starts from the car park and picnic area at Nant Peris, which forms one terminal of the Pen-y-pass park-and-ride service. From the car park it is possible to view the lower slopes of Snowdonia's finest peaks. To the SE, looking directly along the Llanberis Pass is Crib Goch. The lofty SE spur of Glyder Fawr sprawls down on the L, while to the NW are the E slopes of the exile of the Nant Ffrancon, Elidir Fawr. In between these long spurs are the wide green slopes that lead to Y Garn, which are themselves torn by the outcrops of Cwm Cneifio and Esgair y Ceunant.

Leave to the R of the public toilets (on the side of the 'Gents') and follow the narrow, flat path that skirts around a small sheep croft to the R. Within 50 paces you will meet the A4086 from Pen-y-pass to Llanberis, which you should cross and turn R along. Within a few paces turn L to follow a tarmac road that is signposted for the campsite at Cae Gwyn. The tarmac soon gives way to a gravel road bordered by several residential houses and a slate fence on the R. Go through a K-gate and follow this straight gravel track, which is now accompanied by a small brook on the R. A pleasant, quiet campsite occupies the flat grass area on the L, beyond which the large slate tips of the lower slopes of Elidir Fawr dominate. The track bends to the L to a farmhouse and there is a traditional red telephone box on the L here as well. Do not venture towards the farmhouse, since the correct path continues straight on, heading NE through a wide aluminium gate that is located to the L of an old slate building. There is a rusty steel water tank high on the drystone wall to the L, presumably for the sheep or other farm animals. These docile creatures have churned the ground immediately beyond the gate into a quagmire, so take care to walk around this without slipping on the muddy surface!

The gradient increases rapidly now and the wet area quickly disappears. You should head for a gap in the drystone wall ahead. This is followed by about 20 paces of rocky ground, after which the grass continues. There can be a few molehills in this area which have made the ground very uneven. After a few hundred paces a combined fence/wall is crossed by an L-stile. The path is now quite indistinct, but frequent L-stiles and the company of a drystone wall a few hundred metres to the L should assist navigation. The gradient is relentless at this stage and you may soon need to zigzag occasionally to catch your breath. The savage climb has its advantages, though: it will not last too long, and the views improve rapidly to the SW. Dominant in the middle ground are the dark cliffs of Llechog leading up to the summit of Garnedd Ugain. Beyond these sights, in the background, is the gentle arch of Moel Eilio. This segment-shaped mountain increases in grandeur as the climb progresses. When you stop to catch your breath you can catch this view too!

After about 1km (⅝ mile), and having crossed two drystone walls via L-stiles some 200 paces apart, the path flattens as it approaches two L-stiles in rapid succession. These take you over two drystone walls where they join at a corner section (MR 615591). The path is now clearer than it has been previously, but might be indistinct if you are the first to walk this route for some time. The ground is of firm, coarse grass which is stubbly in places and wet where the gradient allows hollows to develop. After the L-stiles there is a short descent to cross a collection of small tributaries that take the surface water from the W slopes of Y Garn. Ahead of you is a good view of these slopes: vast expanses of undulating vegetation and moorland which spell disaster in poor visibility! Fortunately,

the path is straight until the summit of Foel-goch, so if you set your compass to head slightly N of NE, and check this bearing regularly, there should be few problems.

Immediately after the L-stiles you will need to cross quite a large stream. Most of the surrounding area can be very wet and the grass slippery. Be careful not to slip as you look for a suitable crossing place; there are numerous sound rocks but no arranged stepping stones as such. Following this, the ground becomes drier as you climb out of the dip formed by the stream, but the path is still not particularly clear so trust your compass. The gradient eases in comparison with the lower part of the ascent and gives you a chance to marvel at the scenery unfolding around you: Garnedd Ugain and the Snowdon massif to the S, with Elidir Fawr to the N. The grassy slope to the E of you leads to the summit of Y Garn, which is visited later. The present bearing of NE will provide another 1km (⅝ mile) of the grassy ascent of Foel-goch. In very clear weather you may be able to see an L-stile on the horizon, directly ahead on or very near the bearing you are following. On the L is a shallow valley formed by the Afon Gafr and beyond this the small knoll of Esgair y Ceunant. The W slope of this forms one side of a deeper cwm known as Cwm Dudodyn which separates Elidir Fawr beyond.

The open moorland consists mainly of short, stubbly grass and is usually wet. It is secluded and you may see hovering sparrowhawks and other birds of prey as they search for food. After about 1km (⅝ mile) you will reach the saddle between Y Garn and Foel-goch, known as Bwlch y Cywion (MR 628608). This is preceded by the L-stile previously spotted on the horizon, which enables you to cross a fence. Another path crosses the recommended route at the stile going N–S, which you should ignore for now. Walk 20 paces NE to another L-stile which is crammed between a small rock outcrop and the intersection of two fences, forming a corner. From this point the path turns due N, but is very faint because of the extreme weathering on the ridge. You should follow the fence on your L closely, since there are severe drops to the N and NW. Be careful not to snag your clothes on the trailing barbed wire that is detached from the fence here and avoid the ground very close to the fence, which is usually wet and boggy. After about 200 paces you should reach the summit of Foel-goch, which is marked by a small cairn. If the weather is calm, this is a good place to give your legs and feet a rest; if not, you will not stay on the summit for very long! The fence descends ominously out of sight a few metres from the summit and you should take great care if you wish to peep over. The cliffs of the N face of Foel-goch are very treacherous and should be approached with extreme care.

Foel-goch is not as popular as the Glyderau and Tryfan that lie at the head of the Nant Ffrancon, to the SE. It is often ignored, since it is a fair distance from Y Garn and is not easily included in a circular route from Llyn Ogwen. This neglect is undeserved, however, since it is an excellent viewpoint for both the Glyderau and the Carneddau. To the S, Y Garn is the nearest peak, with its significant S slope and N precipice. Further to the E is the rocky morass of Glyder Fawr and then Glyder Fach, and beyond these the character-istic triple peak of Tryfan. Looking due E you will see the massive area of Pen-yr-Ole Wen, which leads to the Carneddau beyond. Nearer to Foel-goch are the peaks of Mynydd Perfedd and Carnedd y Filiast. These are the grassier mountains to the N, whose nearest neighbour is the now familiar Elidir Fawr, to the W.

The way to Y Garn
Allow 1 hour

From Foel-goch, retrace your steps S to the L-stile near the rocky outcrop and, after crossing this, continue S in the direction of Y Garn. The path along the ridge from Foel Goch is spattered with very dark peat deposits, especially at the base of the fence. You will need to cross the fence once again by the L-stile near the rocky outcrop and continue due S. The next 50 paces are relatively flat prior to the final ascent and provide further opportunity for views of Tryfan and the Glyderau. The path is well trodden but not badly eroded. Even in snow the route retains its popularity and the summit path should be clear in most weathers.

It is a narrow, winding track of fine slate pieces. The gradient remains constant and is not too steep, but may limit conversation! The path is reasonably straight for almost 1km ($\frac{5}{8}$ mile), gradually turning to the SE. It follows the edge of the N ridge of Y Garn, high above Cwm Cywion. Quite suddenly, after a kilometre's trudging, the path changes direction to head due S and retreat from the edge of the ridge. At this point (MR 631598) a cairn marks the descent to the floor of the Nant Ffrancon over Pinnacle Crag, which should be disregarded.

Continue on to the summit of Y Garn; cairns mark the path efficiently for use in poor visibility. The summit of Y Garn, at 947m (3,108ft), is crowned by a shallow bowl of rocks, about 3m (10ft) in diameter. The E side of the summit is composed of sheer cliffs and should be respected; the W is very different, being a shallow descent towards Llanberis. The panorama is possibly the most comprehensive in Snowdonia: Elidir Fawr, Mynydd Perfedd, Foel-goch, Carnedd Dafydd, Carnedd Llewelyn, Pen yr Ole Wen, Tryfan, Glyder Fach and Glyder Fawr can all be seen easily from this summit. In good weather, look to the SW, as the summit of Snowdon can be seen only from the summit of Y Garn during this route. Otherwise it is obscured by the huge mass of Garnedd Ugain, just peeping over beyond. Because of the views and the exhilaration of the cliffs, Y Garn is a good place to have a rest and take some refreshment.

The way to Cwm Padrig and back to Nant Peris
Allow 2 hours

From the summit of Y Garn, continue due S down the wide, heavily eroded slope of short grass. There are two almost parallel paths and the choice does not matter, except that one descends further to the E, providing slightly better views of Tryfan. Both paths head due S towards the small lake called Llyn y Cwn (Dog or Hound Lake) that is visible in fine weather. You will cross one of two L-stiles over a new fence and the gradient will reduce gradually. This area is part of the National Trust re-seeding programme and you should obey any relevant signs as to your choice of path at this stage. The

way develops into an excellent repaired track that is easy to follow. The stubbly grass underfoot will eventually change to become rockier and you will soon cross a small stream via a footbridge made of two large rock slabs. This occurs at about 500m (1,641ft) from the summit. Only a short distance further on, you should approach Llyn y Cwn. This lake is about 50m (165ft) across and is situated at the top of Twll Du (Devil's Kitchen) (MR 636585). It is so small and located on such a flat area of land that it is easy almost to walk straight into it in thick mist! The ground surrounding the lake is usually very marshy and wet, as you are now on the saddle between Glyder Fawr and Y Garn and the rainfall from these giants collects here. Views of most of the larger peaks, such as Glyder Fawr and Glyder Fach, are now obscured by their foothills and lower

Tryfan and the Glyderau in the grip of winter.

slopes. However, Tryfan is particularly elegant to the NE, peeping over Twll Du in splendid isolation.

If you keep to the path the route should not get too wet, but this does depend on the time of year and recent weather patterns. Unfortunately, the path from Llyn y Cwn heading WSW is not always obvious and is easily obscured by light snowfalls, which can be present until early May in this area. It is best to leave the lake on a bearing of 260°, with Tryfan to the rear. The terrain is flat for a few hundred paces as you cross the saddle, and you will soon see an L-stile directly ahead which you should make for. The ground gets wetter as the descent steepens slightly and you will need to choose your steps carefully or spend the rest of the day sloshing about in your boots. You will notice here the distinct contrast between the lush, grassy W slopes of Y Garn to the N and the chaotic arrays of Esgair Felen to the S.

Immediately after the L-stile you will cross a small stream via a couple of stepping stones and the path rises up a short bank opposite. It then meanders slightly but, in general, keeps to the bearing, following the stream, the Afon Las, on its R in a shallow ditch. The path is well worn, narrow and mainly of gravel. Along the far bank of the stream runs a new fence, which is crossed by an L-stile after about 100 paces. This L-stile is the first of two crossing the fence which should both be disregarded, as they are more W descents from Y Garn. The stream goes under the fence, which crosses it at right angles to your bearing. The path keeps to the L of the stream and begins to descend more quickly over stubbly grass. From this point, impressive views of Crib Goch are possible to the S. It appears as a very high ridge even from your current position, which is of some altitude. Crib Goch lies to the E of Garnedd Ugain, which is a huge peak on the R.

You will need to cross the fence via an L-stile after a few hundred paces. The terrain changes rapidly now and you must remain vigilant as it weaves in and out of rocky crevices and over grassy plateaux. You will occasionally pass knotted, deformed trees that have been twisted by the wind and seem to be clinging desperately to the little vegetation between rocks and boulders. Indeed, many hang over the deep gully of Cwm Padrig in which the Afon Las runs a few metres below you, to the R. The descent is quick and very soon the waterfalls become visible behind you for the first time. These delightful features will complement much of the remaining route.

If you are following the path by the signs of wear on the rocks and grass, you should come across a small cairn just before a surprising precipice of around 10m (33ft) in height. This is a useful feature which indicates that the correct, safe route is not across the flat, smooth slabs of rock ahead but to the L, going around the small rocky outcrop to bring you out at the bottom of the precipice. Be careful to locate this route since there is otherwise

no easy way down from the precipice, even though storm water has worn a path which can be confusing. This short detour joins a small stream for a few paces, leading you into an area of elderly, twisted hawthorn trees. Many feet have worn a gully into the sandy earth here, which leads to a river to the L. This is a tributary of the Afon Las.

The steady descent may well make your ankles ache and any spot in this area is suitable for a rest, as there is a beautiful view to look at via Cwm Padrig and beyond down the Llanberis Pass towards the coast. Continuing down, the tributary is finally crossed after about 200 paces by means of a substantial aluminium footbridge complete with railings. There is much more short grass on the other side of the bridge, which skirts around a steep rocky outcrop to the L. You may need to use your hands here, because there is a slight drop to the R and the path is narrow for a few paces. After this short, steep section, about 50m (55yd) in length, you will approach a drystone wall which, unfortunately, has several dumped fertilizer bags and their remains at its base. There are also a few slate fence posts by the wall, which crosses in front of you. The path responds with a sharp R turn for a few paces, then turning L to resume its descent again with the wall close by on the L. The ground is quite rocky here and muddy in places. This is particularly true at the L-stile which crosses the intersection of the wall on the L and a fence on the R only a few paces further on. Take care, as there is barbed wire on both sides of the stile and a lot of mud at its base.

After the stile the path follows the route of a derelict fence for a short distance and there are a few silver birch trees lining the banks of the river, which is now quite close to the path. The way is grassier and passes between two ancient gateposts of a drystone wall. The path gradually tracks away from the river and is waymarked by red posts across an undulating meadow. You will leave the meadow via an L-stile over a drystone wall to the right of a small cottage. The next 20 paces are enclosed between a drystone wall and a makeshift fence, which really serves to guide walkers as to the best way across the subsequent small grassy meadow, as the path is otherwise not very clear.

The path follows the drystone wall on the R across this land. Have a good look at the view behind you of the waterfalls and the picturesque cottage on the hillside.

A rust-red K-gate marks the end of the meadow and the beginning of a concrete track which serves another small cottage on the R and is quite enclosed. This track reaches the main A4086 road after about 100 paces. Turn R along this and follow it for almost 1km (⅝ mile) to Nant Peris, remaining vigilant for the Pen-y-pass park-and-ride on the L where the route began. There are many idyllic cottages and farmhouses on the R as you finish your walk that make this final stage very pleasant. There are also the views in the direction of Pen-y-pass to the SE and Llyn Peris to the NW which should not be forgotten, even in a state of fatigue!

Alternative routes

ESCAPES

There are no suitable escapes or short cuts to this walk other than retracing your steps from the summit of Foel Goch to Nant Peris, to omit Y Garn. This might be necessary if the weather deteriorates suddenly, as the ascent of Y Garn can be treacherous in poor visibility.

EXTENSIONS

You may wish to continue due S from Llyn y Cwn up the steep NW slopes of Glyder Fawr to the summit at 999m (3,278ft). From this summit, which is a morass of long flat boulders, you will need to retrace your steps back to Llyn y Cwn to continue along the recommended route.

It is also possible to include Elidir Fawr by heading W from the summit of Foel Goch, which leads you to the summit path of this mountain, at 924m (3,032ft). Once again, you will need to return by the same route to continue the walk as before.

These extensions will add appreciably to the total length of the walk and they should not be undertaken lightly.

The rugged landscape of Cwm Padrig, near Gwastadnant.

61

Route 8: THE NANTLLE RIDGE

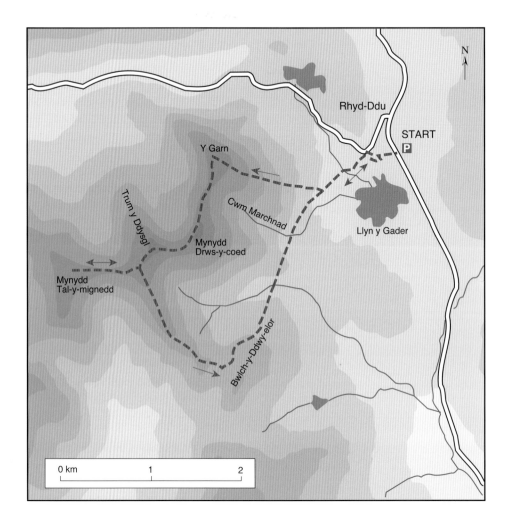

Rhyd-Ddu

START
P

Y Garn

Trum y Ddysgl

Cwm Marchnad

Mynydd
Drws-y-coed

Llyn y Gader

Mynydd
Tal-y-mignedd

Bwlch-y-Ddwy-elor

0 km   1   2

N

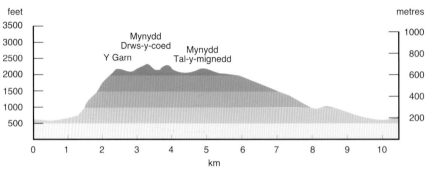

feet   metres

3500   1000

Mynydd
3000   Drws-y-coed

2500   Y Garn   Mynydd   800
                    Tal-y-mignedd
2000   600

1500   400

1000

500   200

0   1   2   3   4   5   6   7   8   9   10

km

Route 8 • The Nantlle Ridge

STARTING LOCATION
Car park at Rhyd-Ddu.
OLM 17/MR 571526.
Capacity for 30 cars.
Public toilets.

ALTERNATIVE STARTING LOCATION
None.

PUBLIC TRANSPORT
Bus route Carnarfon–Beddgelert (along the
    A4085 road).

OVERVIEW/INTEREST
Beautiful, secluded ridge walking with unspoilt
    views of Snowdonia.
Exposed sections providing exhilaration, while
    forestry walking features abundant wild
    flowers.
Visits the Obelisk of Mynydd Tal-y-mignedd.

FOOTPATHS
Paths are very clear throughout.
Much of the route is waymarked.
Exposed sections require great care.
Most of the route is dry and free from mud.

GRADING Difficult
TIME ALLOWANCE 5 hours
DISTANCE
Excluding height 11.5km (7 miles)
TOTAL HEIGHT GAINED 865m (2,855ft)
PRINCIPAL HEIGHTS
Y Garn 633m (2,078ft)
Mynydd Drws-y-coed 695m (2,281ft)
Trum y Ddysgl 709m (2,327ft)
Mynydd Tal-y-mignedd 653m (2,143ft)

The way to Y Garn *Allow 2 hours*

The Nantlle Ridge spans a most beautiful area, approximately 30km (19 miles) square, to the w of Snowdon. This area is isolated, since the Snowdon Horseshoe and the Glyderau shield it from attention. Indeed, travelling by road the most direct routes are via Beddgelert/Carnarfon. However, this does not detract from the quality of walking possible in and around the Nantlle Ridge, nor does it reflect on the beautiful scenery that fills the area in every direction. The Nantlle Ridge is an excellent viewpoint for much of Snowdonia and on a fine day the panorama is quite unique. The Ridge itself is a twisted succession of arêtes and cwms, the latter being the deep bowls carved by glaciers into both sides of it. It is best viewed from either Moel Hebog to the s or from the descent of Snowdon via Allt Maenderyn to the e.

This walk begins at the car park just outside the small village of Rhyd-Ddu. Leave the car park by the most n exit on to the A4085. This disregards the path leaving to the r of the toilets, near to the tourist area map, which in fact leads back towards Rhyd-Ddu. Cross the road immediately, due w, and head for the k-gate opposite. Beyond this, continue along a path of large slates which crosses a meadow of marsh and reeds. There are a couple of farm buildings to your r but, in general, the marsh is very open, stretching to Llyn-y-Gader in the s and Rhyd-Ddu in the n. Directly ahead, looking due w, is the impressive mountain of Y Garn, which defines the most e extent of the Ridge.

After a couple of hundred paces you will pass a large fir tree on the r, and a few paces beyond this the path descends into a small hollow and turns sharp l at a river, the Afon Gwyrfai. The banks of this river are crowded with trees, including hawthorn and other shrubs. The path is accompanied by a few metres of green railings to the r. You should disregard the path which ventures across the stream, through a gate marked

'Private'(!), and instead follow the railings to a K-gate and footbridge, both of which lie a few metres upstream. Continue across the narrow section of grass which follows the footbridge and you will subsequently cross a wide track. This leads to a dwelling by the stream a short distance to the R. The correct path continues straight across this tarmac and up the lush, grassy bank opposite. There is a sign on your L warning of the rigid waymarking system in the area: large white arrows painted on boulders and rocks scattered along the route. In the past the seclusion of the Nantlle Ridge has resulted in poor, indistinct paths and confused walkers have easily become lost. The area now benefits greatly from the comprehensive waymarking and you should be vigilant for the white arrows throughout the walk.

The path continues for a few hundred paces, indicated by waymarkers, until it meets a more established gravel track. It then follows this NW towards a K-gate and L-stile at the corner of the field. At the time of writing, the fence was derelict and neither the stile or gate are required. Continue in the direction of the 'horse and rider' bridlepath sign, heading due W and once again following the obvious waymarkers. This path is wide, clear and dry and proceeds for much of its length between fences or drystone walls. You will pass a large aluminium gate on the R and will also cross a small tributary via a wide footbridge. Follow the widest path to the L-stile which is visible a little way ahead. Beyond this L-stile you will pass between stone gateposts (the gate has long since disappeared), where the path breaks into open country. A few paces after these you will reach a large boulder with two white arrows painted on it, indicating where the path divides. At this position (MR 562522) the gradient increases rapidly to the W as this path tackles the ascent of Y Garn, while the bridlepath heads off SW for the Forest of Beddgelert over flat terrain. The first is the correct path, heading uphill towards two L-stiles about 500 paces up the mountain (the bridlepath forms part of the return route). The path is reasonably clear at this stage, heading due W.

The route steepens drastically now and you will soon leave the arrowed boulder far below. The ascent is very efficient and you might need a rest to catch your breath – it is just as well that the view of Llyn-y-Gader is present to the E to occupy these periods of inactivity. Beyond this, in fine weather the W slopes of Snowdon and Yr Aran dominate, as they will do for much of this route. The path is of short grass and eroded dirt patches, and walking is easy except for the gradient! The E slope of Y Garn is quite dry and relatively free from rocks. Cross the fence ahead by one of the two L-stiles that are available and be sure to check the view behind. At this height (around 500m/1,641ft) the view is transformed into a complete panorama: Moel Eilio in the N, with Foel Gron and Foel Goch slightly to the E beyond, giving way to the dominant Snowdon summit and its S outpost of Yr Aran. In clear weather, the more distant Glyderau and Carneddau can also be seen peeping over these in the background.

Beyond the stiles the path becomes more eroded and steepens considerably. There is now more loose shale underfoot and you may need to use your hands in places. The path will zigzag on its way as it seeks out the easiest route of ascent, traversing to the N and rapidly becoming much more exposed as it approaches the crags of the N face of Y Garn. The exposure increases to the extent that there are sheer cliffs 50m (165ft) high very close to the path. Take care, stay an adequate distance from the edge, and keep hold of youngsters. A few paces further up the mountain you will pass the head of a small cwm, and the terrain will change to a morass of small boulders interspersed with large areas of grass. The gradient reduces as you pass a small cairn and, after crossing a low, partially derelict, drystone wall via an L-stile, you will reach the summit cairn. This lies a few paces to the N. Take great care while on the summit because, as with its namesake of the Nant Ffrancon, there are some very steep gullies to the N of Y Garn. The exposure afforded by these, together with the expansive panorama laid out in front of you, makes Y Garn an impressive summit despite its seclusion. The absence of significant shelter to the N can turn the mountain into a bleak outpost of the Nantlle Ridge if the weather is harsh, and there are a pair of drystone shelters in the form of shallow rings which can provide valuable respite from the relentless wind. However, you may find that other intrepid mountaineers have beaten you to it!

From the summit of Y Garn, the Nantlle Ridge is in view to the SW for the first time. This is an impressive sight and almost alpine in appearance. Nearest is Mynydd Drws-y-coed, which is a rugged, steep-sided peak along the Ridge. Further ahead, there is the grassy dome of Trum y Ddysgl and, beyond this, Mynydd Tal-y-mignedd with its distinct obelisk. The Nantlle Ridge snakes its way SW, such that it is possible to see many of the peaks along the Ridge from Y Garn.

The way to Trum y Ddysgl and on to Mynydd Tal-y-mignedd *Allow 1 hour*

From the summit of Y Garn head due S, along the path which runs to the right of a drystone wall. The rocky terrain of the ascent is not present on the Ridge itself and the path proceeds gently downhill for about 300m (325yd). The ground is usually quite dry and the short grass of this section of the walk gives you an opportunity to recover from the sharp ascent of Y Garn. It also provides respite for the scramble up Mynydd Drws-y-coed, visible ahead. The open grassy ridge continues for about 200 paces beyond the wall. After this the ground changes dramatically, the ridge narrowing considerably with steep sides to the W. These slopes, known as the Clogwyn Marchnad (Market Cliffs) develop quickly from tame screes into severe cliffs and you should be aware of their potential danger. The cliffs are about 200m (656ft) high and intrude very near to the path. The grass of the saddle heading S from Y Garn disappears and the rock pokes through, pointing skywards. The path loses its distinction and you will need to find the most suitable route over the rocks, almost certainly using your hands to steady yourself. Occasionally there are indications of previous footsteps which will guide you, usually just to the L of the Ridge. Do not lose too much height when choosing your route: this will keep the amount of scrambling required to a minimum. There are several precipitous, jutting monoliths of rock that add to the allure of this section.

When you reach the top of Mynydd Drws-y-coed the gradient will reduce and a craggy spur is visible descending steeply to the N; this is called Trum y Ddysgl. The exposed cliffs to the N are still present but the walking is easier because of the reduction in gradient and widening of the path. The way is not very clear, because the ridge is wide enough to disperse the erosion. However, you should continue, not losing too much height, and keeping to the ridge as you proceed. The short grass makes the walking pleasant and your bearing should change gradually from SW to due W as you follow the orientation of the Ridge. After several hundred paces the cliffs cease suddenly, giving way to a wide grassy section of the Ridge. You will need to cross an L-stile and there is a short, gentle ascent to the top of Trum y Ddysgl. This summit is a wide dome that contrasts sharply with the preceding cliffs. It has no cairn and is easily missed. However, it is the highest section of this route (709m/2,327ft) and is worth a break.

In favourable weather conditions, the best views are across the village of Nantlle and beyond to the Menai Straits and Carnarfon in the NW. Nearby, looking due N, there are impressive views of the cliffs of Craig y Bera, the heavily truncated S face of Mynydd Mawr. This mountain is known colloquially as the Elephant Mountain because from the N its silhouette resembles a kneeling elephant.

Continue along the subsequent expansive grassy ridge to the SW which gradually turns to head due W: almost a repeat of the navigation from Mynydd Drws-y-coed. This change of direction coincides with a rapid, grassy descent to the chunky saddle that lies just E of the peak of Mynydd Tal-y-mignedd, which is denoted by the obelist ahead. Along the saddle, the grassy slopes to the S are transformed into craggy screes as you traverse the head of Cwm Dwyfor. From your present position (MR 540514) you can look down into this cwm, which is about 350m (1,148ft) deep. A particularly good view of it is possible (while on another route) from Moel Lefn to the S. The combination of steep slopes on either side of the saddle result in it being narrow and exposed for the next 100 paces or so. To the N you may be able to see the small lake of Llyn Cwmyffynnon in the base of Cwmyffynnon.

The incline that leads to Mynydd Tal-y-mignedd is rugged and occasionally there are rock slabs where old fence posts once stood. One of these posts remains and is rusty and ancient; however, its Liverpool origin can still be discerned from the forged place name on its shaft. The climb is not long and the gradient eases after a few hundred paces. Just after the ancient fence post the path is joined by a drystone wall, and a few paces beyond this lies the summit.

The summit of Mynydd Tal-y-mignedd is marked by a tall obelisk that is reputed to be a Victorian Jubilee memorial erected by local miners in the nineteenth century. It is neat and square, and the more daring visitors to the peak find climbing it irresistible: the view is reported to be spectacular! The base of the memorial is a scattered array of boulders that gives way to a further grassy section of the Ridge, heading due s.

The way to Cwm Pennant and back to Rhyd-Ddu
Allow 2 hours

To complete this circular route of the Nantlle Ridge you need to head due E from the obelisk of Mynydd Tal-y-mignedd, retracing your steps down the grassy slope to the saddle. This descent is easy but is to be savoured, since the climb that follows, up towards Trum y Ddysgl, is steep and strenuous at this stage of the route. However, it is not necessary to climb all the way back to the top of Trum y Ddysgl. Remain vigilant of the terrain to the R as you climb: this slope is streaked with deep, crooked gullies until a very smooth spur leaves to the SE at a height of about 680m (2,598ft). This coincides with Snowdon coming back into view to the E. You should head SE down this spur and follow the eroded shale track that now develops quickly. This descent is quite steep and tends to run away with fatigued legs!

The descent allows views of the Nantlle Ridge to be taken as you leave it behind to the N, while the Snowdon view develops once more, looking E

The majestic Nantlle Ridge stretches out to Trum y Ddysgl.

beyond the intermediate slopes. To the s, the vast valley of Cum Pennant dominates the panorama, to which the coast is a background. Through here the Afon Dwyfor, a shimmering river, snakes its way to the coast beyond Dolbenmaen.

You will make good progress over the terrain of grass and moss, and soon a N arm of the Forest of Beddgelert encroaches to the L. Ahead of you the cluster of peaks around Moel Hebog confuse the view, while the path undulates over the bumpy, wet ground that is familiar in the high-level regions around Beddgelert. After a couple of minor rises, with the forest close to the L, the path descends a steep, winding slope to a boggy saddle known as Bwlch-y-Ddwy-elor (MR 553504). The path ends

at a crossroads with a distinct bridlepath, on to which you should turn L to head NE (the SW direction descends via Cwm Pennant). Almost immediately you will meet a small, rickety gate and the path continues beyond, clear and composed of gravel. The route ventures around a small rise to the L before descending quickly into the forest.

The coniferous trees of the Forest of Beddgelert obscure the sunlight and you are soon shrouded in cool shade. The path becomes rocky and wide and occasionally passes through areas of scattered, felled trees. The track then winds back on itself as it continues to descend through dense forest. After a few hundred paces the path ends abruptly in a junction with a more substantial forest track. The

path is waymarked for Dolbenmaen at this point (MR 556510). Head NE (to the R) on the forestry track. Very soon you will meet a junction where you should turn L. The views of Snowdon continue through the trees and bushes to the E and the track enters an area of the forest where there are fewer trees. The track then follows a straight course for several hundred paces, remaining NE, until it reaches another junction and a concrete bridge in an open area of the woodland. At this position (MR 557513) you should head NNE along a narrow path through the scrubland just beyond the bridge. This path covers a short distance before crossing the forestry path again. After this it continues on the same bearing up a slight incline.

The gradual climb crosses terrain of lush grass that is bordered by young deciduous trees, including birch and ash. It then passes between ancient stone gateposts at the head of the rise before beginning the gradual descent, still heading NNE. The sweeping valley of Betws Garmon opens up ahead, with fantastic views of Llyn y Gader and Snowdon most prominent. The path keeps a straight course and descends very gradually. Do not lose too much height or descent directly towards the lake, since the lower regions are very wet and are used by cattle. The path is very clear and heads for an L-stile over a wire fence, which denotes the border between the forest and the open country to the N.

The continuation path remains clear and soon crosses the flatter terrain to the east of Cwm Marchnad. This narrow cwm is host to a small, lively river that descends via idyllic pools and waterfalls from the peak of Mynydd Drws-y-coed. There is a small cluster of boulders for use as stepping stones across the stream. From Cwm Marchnad the path becomes more eroded and consists mainly of shale, sometimes following deep grooves in heavy soils. You will need to pass between a couple of weighted gates after about 500 paces, where the path remains clear, far above Llyn y Gader and to the L of the cattle land surrounding the lakeside. There are also a couple of busy brooks to be crossed before the white arrow waymarking system begins once again. This will lead you back to the large boulder where the route struck off for Y Garn earlier in your walk. From here you should

The sweeping spurs of the Nantlle Ridge lead to the coast.

descending, as the surface of the path is loose and approaches areas of some exposure. Further on, you can omit Mynydd Tal-y-mignedd and descend immediately via the spur to the head of Cwm Pennant, continuing, as recommended, through the forest back to Rhyd-Ddu.

EXTENSIONS

A considerable extension to this route is possible which is only advisable for strong walkers in the summer months, when there is ample daylight. From the obelisk at Mynydd Tal-y-mignedd you should head off ssw down the ensuing wide, grassy ridge. This proceeds towards the craggy outcrops of Craig Pennant and Trwyn y Craig in the distance, looking sw. The grassy ridge soon narrows and steepens greatly as the path descends over rocky ground to reach the saddle of Bwlch Dros-bern. From this saddle there is a considerable climb up the ridge, along the top of Craig Pennant and over an expanse of rocks which leads to a nameless summit at 734m (2,063ft) (MR 525503). There is a rugged shelter on the top and several derelict obelisks. From here you should continue across the lengthy, high-level moonscape of Craig Cwm Silyn. The path crosses a fence and drystone wall by means of a P-stile and then keeps to the R of the wall for the next 1km (⅝ mile). You will eventually reach the summit of Garnedd Goch, at 700m (2,297ft), by continuing along the ridge to the sw. There are interesting views to both sides: to the SE Moel Hebog and the associated peaks are dominant, while to the NW you look down over Llynnau Cwm Silyn towards the village of Nantlle itself. There are, of course, the views of the Nantlle Ridge itself from this s outpost.

From Garnedd Goch you need to retrace your steps all the way back to Mynydd Tal-y-mignedd, so think carefully before attempting this extension! In practice, the last climb up to the obelisk of Mynydd Tal-y-mignedd can be gruelling, but there is plenty of time for recuperation on the gentle return route through the Forest of Beddgelert, as recommended in the standard route.

retrace your steps back along the waymarked footpaths that cross the marshy farmland N of Llyn y Gader, to the car park. The car park is usually very quiet, allowing you to view the Nantlle Ridge once more while easing off your boots! You may also wish to seek refreshment from the small hotel in Rhyd-Ddu to complete your walk.

Alternative routes

ESCAPES

This walk is quite short but is strenuous in places. It is possible to curtail it by simply returning from the summit of Y Garn, descending by the way of ascent, to the car park. Be sure to take care when

Route 9: TREFOR AND YR EIFL

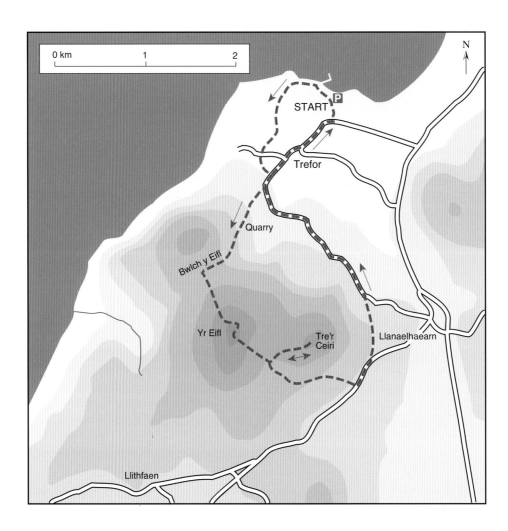

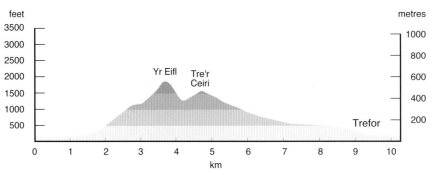

Route 9 • Trefor and Yr Eifl

STARTING LOCATION
Car park at Trefor Harbour.
OLSR 123/MR 375472.
Capacity for 30 cars.
No toilets.

ALTERNATIVE STARTING LOCATION
None.

PUBLIC TRANSPORT
None.

OVERVIEW/INTEREST
Explores the hills surround the sleepy village of
    Trefor on the Lleyn Peninsula.
Passes the pretty harbour and pier of Trefor.
Spectacular coastal scenery.
Features include a disused granite quarry, the
    ancient fort of Tre'r Ceiri and the Cwm Pottery.

FOOTPATHS
Paths are clear throughout.
Avoid quarry ruins.
Some parts of the route are severely eroded,
    others follow quiet hill roads.
Waymarking is minimal.

GRADING   Moderate
TIME ALLOWANCE   4½ hours
DISTANCE
Excluding height   9.5km (5.9 miles)
TOTAL HEIGHT GAINED   679m (2,241ft)
PRINCIPAL HEIGHTS
Yr Eifl 564m (1,851ft)
Tre'r Ceiri 485m (1,592ft)

The way to Yr Eifl
Allow 2 hours

This walk starts from the large free car park at the seaside in Trefor, and to find it you need to look out for a small turning to the R that leaves before you reach the village centre. One side of the car park is bordered by a short row of cottages, while the other has a flimsy fence with mudflats beyond. After the mudflats there is a small harbour and jetty; there are usually a few boats awaiting high tide in the harbour and you can walk along the jetty to the small modern pier if you wish. The coastline sweeps away to the NE along lengthy stretches of sand towards the SW side of Anglesey. The view in this direction is complemented by the rounded hills to the E of Trefor which form a very distinctive triplet of peaks: Moel Pen-llechog (297m/975ft), Gyrn Ddu (522m/1,713ft) and Gyrn Goch (492m/1,614ft). To the S the view is dominated by the sharper hills of Yr Eifl.

Leave the car park by the tarmac track that heads for the jetty, past an information panel that recounts the history of the harbour, and on to the NW. The track is flat and the sea breeze is refreshing as you marvel at the beautiful views all around. You will pass a few boulders on the R and will soon reach the edge of the harbour. The route continues through a gate marked 'No parking' (you can push past without opening it) and on to deep, fine sand. This only lasts a few paces before gravel is reached. From this position (MR 374474) you can see the pier, which was previously hidden by the jetty. The harbour and jetty were originally built and used by the quarry company; the quarry was opened in 1850 and the harbour was constructed a few years later. At first horses pulled the carts of granite down from the mountain and along the track you are now following. Then the industrial revolution brought steam engines, before the twentieth century used trucks for the purpose. The quarry closed in 1971 and the harbour and jetty have since been modernized and altered, while the pier is a later development. The quarry supplied granite to much of the UK, a legacy evident from the apparent missing section of the N peak of Yr Eifl.

Follow the gravel track along the sea front to the W, past a small boatyard declaring 'Boats for sale'. The track crosses a busy river via a wide bridge made of old railway sleepers and rusty iron plates. A few paces after this it turns to the SW and heads away from the coast but remains flat and pleasant. There is granite and other quarry debris to the L with gorse and scrubland beyond, while the view ahead is dominated by the peaks of Yr Eifl. After a few hundred paces the path becomes more sheltered and there are some buildings to the R. A short distance further on you will reach a wide, white gate near to a farm on the L. Continue on along the track, through the gate, past the farm and up the slight incline. The track becomes shrouded in thick hedge and trees. Be vigilant, as the farm has pigs and they tend to peer through the thick hedge to the L. There are some rare breeds and they might surprise you with a grunt!

A few hundred paces further on the track leads into a large gravel area which is part of the local bus station. The route acquires a slightly industrial flavour as you continue, keeping to the R and passing the Beryn Garage. The track leaves the area near to a large building with bricked-up windows and begins the long ascent of the old quarry cartway. This section is very straight and at the top of the ascent, some distance away, you will be able to see the derelict quarry buildings and machinery. Gorse grows raggedly on both sides of the loose tarmac. There is a road below which you will soon cross via a bridge; this leads to the Plas Yr Eifl Hotel (marked 'Inn' on the map).

Immediately after the bridge you should leave the track via a narrow path that snakes around the L side of the bridge to the road below. Although there is a path shown on the map that continues towards Yr Eifl through the quarry, this right of way is not supported and is potentially dangerous. Hence, it is necessary to cross country to ascend the cwm between the quarry mountain and Yr Eifl itself. The narrow path meets the road, but after a few paces it leaves to the R through a red K-gate at the top of a few overgrown steps. This leads to a small area of pasture. Follow the path around the perimeter of the field to the R, where it will meet an L-stile. In the next field you should follow the perimeter to the L to another L-stile, before which you will be able to hear a bubbling stream in a natural recess beneath your

feet. Suddenly the nature of the route is changed from vast, open views of Trefor and the surrounding hills to small meadows and hedgerows. The stile leaves you in an inclined tarmac lane between thick hedges.

Turn R along the road and head uphill. The road weaves upwards and you will be able to see the quarry buildings once again to your R. After only a few paces on the steep tarmac the lane bends sharply to the L and heads downhill, while your continuation route is a grassy lane which heads off SW, uphill. There is a signpost in the hedge to the R advertising the Cwm Pottery further down the lane; you should ignore this for now and follow the grassy lane.

The terrain changes once again from MR 268462. The path proceeds along mossy ground that cushions your feet. This way blends with the hedgerows and drystone walls on either side, which provide shelter. There is an old bed on the L followed by a silver-grey K-gate. The path steepens and narrows, and tracks leave to the R and L which should be disregarded in favour of the SW bearing. Gradually the sheltered nature of this section of the route is exchanged for the open moorland of the lower sections of Yr Eifl. On one of the author's visits to this hillside he was greeted by a white long-horned goat, who scuttled off down the snow-covered hillside soon afterwards.

The path adopts a groove on the side of the cwm, below the jagged peak of the quarry mountain to the R. After the next gate (small and red) the path leaves the channel and heads off into open country. You should keep to the fence on the R, continuing to climb to the SW. The view from this hillside is fantastic: looking across the scattering of houses around Trefor, the hills opposite provide a pleasant background to the nearby gorse and heather that sweep into the cwm to your L. As you ascend, small screes begin to approach the path and soon you will be able to see the radio mast near the old quarry site. After a further few hundred paces, the gradient begins to reduce as you reach the head of the cwm. To the L the large lumbering mass of Yr Eifl grows in perspective; you might be able to hear the clay-pigeon shooting range echoing across the valley in this region.

The top of the cwm ends in a saddle called Bwlch yr Eifl. This is a wide, inclined area of heather that is woven with a confused tangle of paths and sheep tracks. Do not be tempted to head off due s too early on the ascent of Yr Eifl, as the terrain is tricky and will slow you down; instead, continue sw. After a few hundred yards you will reach a wider gravel path that is used to serve the radio mast and station from the village of Llithfaen in the s. This path forms a crossroads nearby on a flat part of the saddle (MR 362454). You should turn L here, heading SSE for the summit of Yr Eifl. The path is narrower than the gravel preceding it, but is well worn and clear throughout the heather. It climbs quickly and you will soon leave Bwlch yr Eifl far below.

The path to the summit of Yr Eifl is not shown on the map but is the best route from the N. After only a few hundred paces you will reach scattered rubble sections that dominate the upper slopes where the heather is less prevalent. These rubble areas develop into large areas of huge slabs and boulders and the path loses definition. You should continue climbing. Yr Eifl has an oval-shaped summit lying NE–SW and you might reach the NE end of it by following the path. If this is the case, the summit cairn and triangulation point can be found a few paces along the summit to the SW. There is also a small shelter near the summit.

Yr Eifl is an unusual mountain. It is not as characteristic as the peak near the quarry in the N and lacks features by comparison. The wide summit restricts views in most directions, but the variety of the scenery compensates for this. To the W, the deep blue waters of Caernarfon Bay shimmer beyond the quarry, while to the E the rippled landscape of Snowdonia may be observed in fine weather. Looking SW the long beaches around Morfa Nefyn are in view. As you begin your descent the landscapes will improve with the appearance of nearby hills, specifically Tre'r Ceiri.

Sunrise over Yr Eifl.

The way to Tre'r Ceiri and back to Trefor

Allow 2½ hours

Viewed from Trefor, the Yr Eifl range appears as a high ridge with the truncated peak near the quarry lying to the SW end. The S edge of the range can be reached by walking along the ridge but this does require scrambling over large areas of boulders. Instead, it is better to descend to the SE. There is a clear path that loses height rapidly, while views of the hills of Tre'r Ceiri (E) and Mynydd Carnguwch (SE) dominate. Since Yr Eifl is relatively small (564m/1,851ft) you will find the path becomes less steep and follows to the R of a drystone wall. The loose rocks recede and are replaced by heather and sodden peat, and you will pass a large outcrop of rocks to the R. It crosses a wire fence near to the wall by a makeshift stile of raised rocks on either side. The path eventually meets the wall at an L-stile, which you should cross over.

The path from the L-stile is shown on the map. It passes near to a stonemason's hut by the wall and heads off down the slope to the SE. The terrain is easy in this section, consisting of short grass and patches of heather. Before striking off for the descent, it is worth climbing the short distance to the summit of Tre'r Ceiri via a path that heads off to the NE. This hill is smaller (485m/1,592ft) than the main summit of Yr Eifl, but has the distinction of being the site of an ancient fort. This becomes evident as you approach, since there are remnants of thick walls around the top. There is also a weatherproof information display nearby.

The fort at Tre'r Ceiri has uncertain origins but was established before the Romans reached the area in AD 78. It is believed that use of it declined in the fourth century. The walls are impressive, being quite intact in places; the summit of Tre'r Ceiri lies to the NE end of the high land. Good views of the SE aspect of Tre'r Ceiri are possible later in the walk. From the summit you should descend by the same path of ascent to the SW. There is another path that heads S from the SW entrance to the fort, but this has been very badly eroded and is a scar on the hillside. There are barriers to prevent its use and encourage vegetation to reclaim it. As you continue your descent, you will turn to head due

E and after a few hundred paces will meet another L-stile. The terrain continues to be gentle, with the expanses of ferns nearby turning a vivid orange in the autumn. You will soon be able to hear the traffic using the road in the valley ahead, while to the N the ancient ramparts of the fort can be seen above the path. The route then turns to head SE once again and follows a wide grassy path to the R of a drystone wall. This ends among some small sheepfolds near to the wall and a rickety gate. Beyond this gate there is a short meadow which you should cross, keeping to the wall on the L. There is a disused L-stile to the L also, just before a rusty red K-gate, after which a few steps lead you to the B4417. There is also a waymarker to the L here – one of the first seen on this route.

Walk about 300m (325yd) along the road, heading NE. It is busy, especially in summer because of Tre'r Ceiri, so take care and use the wide grass verge on the R. Just before the road descends decisively toward Llanaelhaearn a footpath leaves to the L, so look out for it. It is waymarked 'For Trefor' and starts as a few steps up to a red K-gate. The path heads due N across an open field and follows a faint ridge in the terrain. This field was occupied by some inquisitive horses when the author last visited and you will pass a horse trough along the way. Head for the L-stile that lies at the top of the field by following the perimeter and keeping well clear of the horses. There are some buildings beyond a fence to the R.

After the L-stile, which crosses a wire fence, you will be in a steeply inclined field that lies along an E–W ridge which tends to collect snow in winter. You should continue N; there are traces of tracks and paths, as this field is sometimes used for clay-pigeon shooting and you will spot the scattered remnants of the clay discs used in this sport on the ground close to the path. In winter the steep gradient of this field can make it slippery and awkward to cross. It is not much further before you meet the fence with the minor road that links Llanaelhaearn with Trefor. Follow the fence to the NW until you meet a K-gate, which leads you to the tarmac road back to Trefor.

The road to Trefor is very narrow and quiet, and winds its way around the N reaches of Yr Eifl, up

The tiny harbour at Trefor.

and down over the undulated terrain. The w view is dominated by the sweeping slopes of the hills, with the upper rocky sections towering beyond. As you continue you will notice many footpaths leaving to the R. These are short cuts for Trefor, but do not save much time or distance in comparison with the road. After 0.5km (⅓ mile) you will descend into a sheltered fold of the hillside and the road passes between two old buildings. This is the Cwm Pottery (signposted earlier in the route) and is worth a visit. There is usually a menagerie of animals around, including peacocks and rabbits, while a bubbling river races under the road nearby. The road climbs out of the cwm and reaches the place where the route struck off earlier, up the cwm for Yr Eifl. This time, follow the road as it bends round to the R and heads NE for the village. You will pass a side road to the L which heads for the Plas Yr Eifl Hotel which you should disregard and will then enter the village proper.

Trefor is a pretty village with much character provided by its authentic backstreets and the smell of coal fires in winter. Walk through the village;

you will pass a small foodstore at a junction where you should join the main street and follow it L as it heads out of town past a few pretty houses and cottages. Just before you leave the residential area altogether, a small road leaves to the L that is waymarked for the beach 'Traeth'. Follow this down the short, steep descent to the quayside and back to the car park.

Alternative routes

ESCAPES
This walk is short and therefore no short cuts are recommended.

EXTENSIONS
Although there are many hills near to Yr Eifl, such as Mynydd Carnguwch and the Gyrn Ddu range, these are best tackled as separate routes from Trefor or Llanaelhaearn.

Route 10: CARNEDD MOEL SIABOD

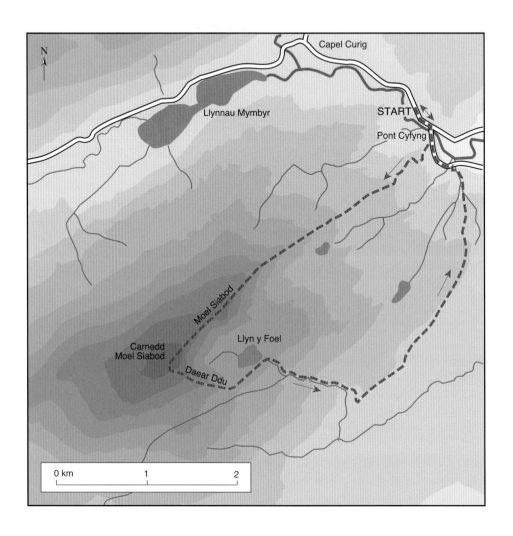

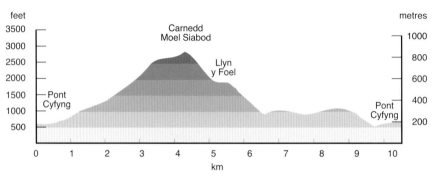

5

CENTRAL SNOWDONIA

Route 10 • Carnedd Moel Siabod

STARTING LOCATION
Car park at Tyn-y-coed Hotel (seek permission).
OLM 17/MR 732573.
No toilets.

ALTERNATIVE STARTING LOCATION
Cyfyng Falls MR 734572 (no parking).

PUBLIC TRANSPORT
Bus route Bangor–Betws-y-coed (along the A5 road).

OVERVIEW/INTEREST
Unusual and demanding ridge walking, descending via the exhilarating Daear Ddu ridge.
Views of the Rhinogyll range and Glyderau.
Passes through deserted forest and beautiful open country, with derelict quarrying settlements of historical interest.

FOOTPATHS
Paths are mostly clear, but careful navigation is required on the summit ridge and in the forest.
Higher sections pass areas of some exposure where care must be taken.
Can be wet and boggy throughout the route.

GRADING Difficult
TIME ALLOWANCE 5½ hours
DISTANCE
Excluding height 11.25km (7 miles)
TOTAL HEIGHT GAINED 872m (2,862ft)
PRINCIPAL HEIGHTS
Carnedd Moel Siabod 872m (2,862ft)

The way to Carnedd Moel Siabod

Allow 3 hours

Carnedd Moel Siabod, better known simply as Moel Siabod, hangs over the village of Capel Curig to the sw and is set aside from the Glyderau and Carneddau, several kilometres E of Betws-y-coed. Heading SE from the Menai Straits, Moel Siabod is famous for its views of the Snowdon Horseshoe to the w and the Glyderau to the NW. However, this notoriety also extends to the very wet, marshy slopes to the E and the swarms of persistent flies in summer. Moel Siabod has an extensive, craggy ridge almost 2km (1¼ miles) long that ends in a steep cwm encircling Llyn y Foel, and the SE slopes of the mountain are partially covered in forestry. This variety of fine scenery is strong justification for attempting the following route.

To begin the walk, park at the large car park opposite the Tyn-y-coed Hotel in Capel Curig; the hotel has a full-size Victorian stagecoach outside it. Walk a couple of hundred metres down the A5 (s) to the Cyfyng Falls and take the small road to the right through Pont Cyfyng. Go over the bridge and, ignoring the path leaving immediately afterwards, walk for about 100 paces until you see a path leaving to the R up a steep hill. Follow this as it becomes shrouded in pine forest and rises sharply out of the valley. Be aware that motor vehicles use this track in order to access the farms at the base of Moel Siabod. The path has large signs restricting vehicular access, since it is private except for walkers.

Moel Siabod from Dolwyddelan.

As the path breaks into the open after about 400m (433yd) it also flattens out and winds steadily amid ferns. The way bends sharply to the R, and as it curves back to the L you will pass through a farmyard. The terrain is now mainly of ferns and bracken and the path is of loose slate. After a few hundred paces you will need to cross over a fence via an L-stile and proceed up the (now relentless) incline. Disregard the private path which leaves to the L through a gate, as it leads to dangerous quarry ruins, and head SW. At this stage there are impressive views ahead (SW) of Moel Siabod and to your R (NW) of the distant Carneddau and the Glyderau. As you gain height you should be able to see the distinctive Pen Llithrig-y-Wrach to the NE, which forms the N side of Llyn Cowlyd. The country then becomes more open and the gradient reduces. There are plenty of sheep (usually) and the occasional reeds indicate the marshy ground on either side of the path. You will need to use another L-stile by a derelict building and should ignore any minor paths leaving to the L. The straightness of the path is so distinctive that it is obvious to follow.

After about 0.5km (⅓ mile) on this straight path, you need to locate an L-stile to the R fed by a lesser path leading in the direction of the main ridge and higher ground to the SW. Leave the main path here (MR 724563) via this L-stile before continuing up the mountain. This path is much more rocky and uneven and is consequently less distinct. It leads through a great deal of heather and passes some old iron parts of a makeshift fence to the L. Further ahead the lower stretches of the ridge begin as a large groove in the mountainside that may well have been part of a quarry cart track in the past. Pass through a dilapidated drystone wall and follow the groove – the ascent is best on the R side as the L and centre areas can be very boggy and wet. There are large slabs of rock to the R which bear the wounds of past glacial action.

After only a few hundred metres, the path leads to more rugged terrain of steep scree and loose rock, and you will need to use your hands to pick your way over the most suitable route. Quite quickly, however, the gradient reduces and you will reach a plateau. From here you can see distinctive sections of stepped rock to the NW, which are presumably further evidence of quarrying in the last century. Ahead of you the E end of the Moel Siabod ridge should be visible, consisting of a confused array of boulders and slabs. A small cairn indicates the way to this section of the mountain.

For most of the ridge of Moel Siabod, it is advisable to follow a route just to the R (N) side as you proceed SW. This is because the ridge is not easily negotiated due to the uneven rocky terrain. In addition, there are two very deep gullies in the ridge that cannot be seen easily and pose a formidable hazard. By keeping to the R you should find the walking is improved by the grassier terrain, and the gullies are avoided. However, do not lose too much height, since the summit is a further 1km (⅝ mile) ahead. The path on this ridge is not distinct and is not marked on the map. Despite this, Moel Siabod is a popular mountain and the recommended route continues SW. This bearing is almost parallel to the A4086, which can be seen in the valley to the N. The rocky ground makes walking quite difficult and you may find the rocks very slippery in wet weather. The first stages of the ridge are the worst in this respect, and as you reach the summit you will find the terrain easier. This is due to the more definite path that has been eroded into the mountainside in the later stages.

The summit of Moel Siabod is a broad dome, flanked to the S by steep rock faces and a compact ridge known as Daear Ddu. There is a large cairn and a triangulation point, and a few paces beyond these a drystone shelter. Views from the summit on a fine day are superb. The Snowdon Horseshoe can be seen to the NW but you may need to leave the summit a few metres to the N to get the best view. To the R of this, the distinctive pointed summit of Tryfan can be seen peeping between Glyder Fach and the Carneddau on the horizon. Looking SE there is a different selection of features: the foreground is made up of the rolling countryside around Dolwyddelan with its famous castle, while the distant view looks toward Carnedd-y-Filiast and the Berwyns. The Moelwyns, Moel Hebog and Cnict dominate the SW.

The way via Daear Ddu to the forest

Allow 1 hour

The walk continues down the E ridge of Daear Ddu. From the summit, walk about 50 paces to the E and descend via a steep gully. A path can be followed easily in the gully, but the steepness and ruggedness of the ridge can make this descent complicated. The higher sections of the ridge make a good viewpoint for the lake, called Llyn-y-Foel, which it skirts around. To the SW the distinctive shape of Cnict can be seen, and beyond this Llyn Trawsfynydd, with the characteristic power station building. The Rhinogyll lie beyond. To the SE the expansive forestry areas that surround Betws-y-coed are also visible.

Daear Ddu is short but still presents considerable exposure and the dangers inherent in this. Keep rigidly to the path and do not venture too far for views. The path is evident from the visible erosion

Descending Daear Ddu to Llyn-y-Foel.

on the rocks and rambles its way down the ridge as a river might do. The views that accompany this quick descent, of the Siabod massif to the NW and the panorama of the S, make it a particularly satisfying section of the route. The foot of the ridge joins the S lakeside which is a suitable place for a break. The lake is very clear and tranquil, and there is a small beach at the most W point which is set against some drystone structures that are possibly old dam workings. The route continues from this point, through these workings and to the SE. The path passes through dense ferns, while the small river from the lake descends quickly to the R through a series of small waterfalls. Both the path and river head for the large forest to the E. This is a very pretty part of the walk. To the rear stands Moel Siabod, a huge haunting massif, while the descent is decorated with heather and gorse complemented by the boiling waterfalls.

The path deviates away from the river, only to join it once more near to the edge of the forest, to the SE of Moel Siabod. Here (MR 721545), it crosses the river at some large stepping stones and then crosses a fence by means of an L-stile. This fence constitutes the boundary where the forest begins and the open lower hills of Moel Siabod end. Finding your way in the forest can be difficult, as the path becomes unclear in places. The important thing to remember is to stay reasonably close to the river as the path runs roughly parallel to it. Eventually, after about 100 paces in dense forest, the path widens and flattens out into a wide avenue. Disregard any paths leaving to either side and keep the river to your L. At the end of this avenue the river bends to the R and you can cross it easily by the wide stepping stones. Beyond this there is a steep, grassy bank which leads to the wide circular cul-de-sac of a forestry commission track. From here, orientation is much easier. Follow the forestry track SE until it meets a crossroads, where you should turn L to head NE. At the author's last visit, this area of the forest was quite open as the trees are young and short. There is an assortment of wild flowers on the sides of the track among older fallen trees.

On the return from Moel Siabod.

The way back to Pont Cyfyng *Allow 1½ hours*

The forestry path climbs steadily, crossing a flat region and some crossroads before meeting another forestry track after little more than 500 paces. Turn L here and follow the subsequent track NE. Disregard a forestry track which leaves to the L shortly after this junction, since it brings you back into the forest. You should find that the correct path leads to open country after about 100 paces.

The path is wide and clear and leaves you free to admire the surroundings. To your L, a steeply inclined field obscures part of Moel Siabod beyond it. To your R, the small hill of Mynydd Cribau can be seen, with the forest of Betws-y-coed visible beyond it. After 1km (⅝ mile) the path deviates slightly to the L and starts to descend into the valley towards Pont Cyfyng.

As you continue to follow the gentle descent, you will soon enter the small wood that surrounds Pont Cyfyng. This consists predominantly of oak trees. Ignore any lesser paths leaving to either side. Your continuation path will bend around to the N and then crosses a small river via an almost hidden bridge. Immediately following this the path reaches a gate and an L-stile. Having negotiated these, the track descends quickly and passes close to the L of a house and an inconspicuous chapel. Here the track meets the tarmac road, where you should turn L. This road passes a few houses set in the wood before being joined to the L by the steeply descending path that you followed at the outset. From here, retrace your steps over the small bridge and N along the A5. This will take you to the car park and perhaps some well-earned refreshment.

Alternative routes

ESCAPES
This route cannot be shortened substantially because of the predominance of derelict quarries and their inherent hazards. Much of the area has restricted access because of this.

EXTENSIONS
No extensions are recommended.

Route 11: CWM NANTCOL AND THE RHINOGYLL

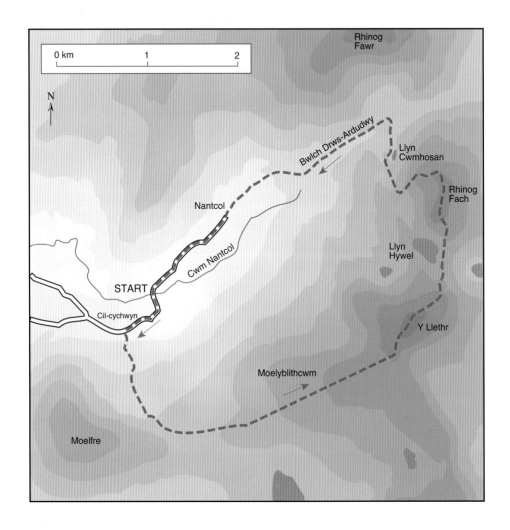

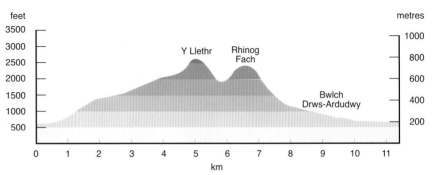

6

SOUTHERN SNOWDONIA

Route 11 • Cwm Nantcol and the Rhinogyll

STARTING LOCATION
Car parking in Cwm Nantcol (small charge).
OLM 18/MR 634263.
Capacity for 10 cars.
No toilets.

ALTERNATIVE STARTING LOCATION
None.

PUBLIC TRANSPORT
None.

OVERVIEW/INTEREST
Explores a beautiful isolated valley in the Rhinog
    National Nature Reserve, with abundant
    wildlife.
Easily extended to include further interest.

FOOTPATHS
Mixture of moorland and steep, rocky paths.
Short sections cross coarse screes.
Some precipitous edges require care and respect.
Compass is essential.
For much of the route the path is permissive and
    should be respected.

GRADING   Moderate
TIME ALLOWANCE   5½ hours
DISTANCE
Excluding height   11.5km (7.2 miles)
TOTAL HEIGHT GAINED   798m (2,617ft)
PRINCIPAL HEIGHTS
Y Llethr 756m (2,481ft)
Rhinog Fach 712m (2,337ft)

The way to Y Llethr   *Allow 2½ hours*

The Rhinogyll are the two rugged mountains that
stand either side of the head of the idyllic valley of
Cwm Nantcol. Geographically, they form the
middle section of the scarred spine of a long ridge
that stretches from the Mawddach Estuary in the S
to the Vale of Ffestiniog in the N. To the E of this
ridge is a massive expanse of flatter land that is
partly forested and almost free from roads and
habitation. In summer, this area is renowned
among walkers for its barren character and absence
of running water. This reputation has led to it being
considered a deserted and remote place. To the W
of the ridge is a large area of land that descends to
the coast and the resorts of Barmouth, Llanbedr and
Harlech. This land is scored by a number of long
valleys, of which two – Cwm Nantcol and Cwm
Bychan – are particularly beautiful. In contrast to
their benign appearance from the map and
intermediate height, the Rhinogyll and their
neighbours are hewn from notoriously difficult
terrain that demands considerable physical effort.
This area is part of a National Nature Reserve and is
to be kept as isolated as possible to retain the rare
wildlife habitat.

   To begin the walk you should park in Cwm
Nantcol. There are two suitable places: near the
farm at Cil-cychwyn (ME 634259) and further
along the narrow tarmac road beyond the Afon
Cwmnantcol (MR 634263), close to a mature crab
apple tree. In both cases the parking is on the grass
to either side of the track and is signposted. There

is a small charge (50p at the time of writing) to be left in a small cup by the sign. Space is very limited, so get there early.

On your first visit to Cwm Nantcol you may well be overwhelmed at the glorious scenery that lies hidden a few miles E of Llanbedr. There is virtually no traffic and the only sounds are the mountain breeze, a few baaing sheep and possibly some cattle calling from across the valley. If you look to the NE the Rhinogyll are visible, standing as sentries to either side of the saddle of Bwlch Drws-Ardudwy. To the E is the long, smoother mountain of Y Llethr, and turning to the SW is the more isolated lump of Moelfre. The narrow tarmac road winds gently across the valley towards this hill and guides you for the first stage of the walk.

From the car park at MR 634263 you should follow the road downhill to the S. It crosses the Afon Cwmnantcol at a small, modern bridge, the river flowing both narrow and smooth among reeds and marsh grass. After this short downhill section the road climbs gently in straight sections between drystone walls and wire fences, before reaching the farm at Cil-cychwyn. This is the place where additional parking may be found near one of the barns on the L. Along the tarmac road several footpaths leave from either side, which are waymarked clearly. These should be disregarded until you are several hundred paces from the farm. At this point (MR 631257) you should take a waymarked footpath which leads off to the S just beyond a cattle-grid and L-stile. The clear, wide

path leads up a grassy, inclined meadow that is speckled with clumps of reeds.

The grassy path maintains a straight course and is lightly rutted from farm vehicle use. After a few hundred paces it deviates to the L of a derelict drystone wall and heads for an L-stile over another wall. Excellent views are possible to the NE, with the Rhinogyll and Y Llethr forming the background to the gentle valley of Cwm Nantcol. The long, grassy E spur of Moelfre accompanies the climb to the R. The last few steps before the L-stile are steep and slippery in the wet and there is a broken metal gate on the L. After the L-stile the path changes direction to head SE for the next few hundred paces. As you continue up the incline you will cross a stone footbridge over a noisy, fast-flowing

stream. The path remains clear and is occasionally waymarked by substantial yellow posts. These are particularly useful further on, where the terrain becomes more rocky and the path loses some definition.

Presently you will come over a slight rise as the path heads for another drystone wall ahead. There is no L-stile by which to cross this wall, but there is an obvious place where the wall is derelict and broken down. The upper E slopes of Moelfre are quite rocky and are strewn with light screes that encroach upon the land to the R, with some considerable crags on the higher ground. You will pass another yellow waymarking post and might notice that the ground becomes more boggy and wet as the gradient relaxes slightly. Directly ahead, looking SSE, there is a distinctive upright stone on the horizon. The path heads for this, passing several trickling brooks on the way. Beyond the stone, the gradient reduces further and you should make for a large deliberate gap in the next drystone wall. After this you cross a small meadow enclosed by walls, heading towards an L-stile opposite. This area is host to many toadstools and other fungi in the autumn. As the gradient reduces and you reach the saddle between the eastern spur of Moelfre and Moelyblithcwm, further views are possible to the SE of the Diffwys (750m/2,461ft). There is a rusty gate to the R of the L-stile which crosses the last wall of this part of the ascent.

You should now be near the drystone wall, just short of the saddle described earlier at MR 636246. From this position, head just N of due E, going in the direction of a pronounced corner in the distinctive drystone wall that descends SW along Moelyblithcwm. This is obvious in good visibility, but in mist a compass is essential; make sure not to lose any height. The ground is good and dry, although the clumps of grass can make parts of the walk difficult. As you track across the moorland you might pass a small overgrown sheep enclosure at about half-way. Breathtaking views of Moelfre are possible from this position, looking W. This hill is impressive because it is isolated from nearby peaks and is therefore distinctive, even though it

Early morning mist over the Rhinogyll.

85

is comparatively small. As you continue towards the wall to the E, you will cross many sheep tracks and must keep faithfully to your bearing. After 0.5km (⅓ mile) you wil reach the drystone wall. Follow to the R of it, where there is a clear path of worn grass and exposed peat. This climbs relentlessly up Moelyblithcwm for the next 1.5km (1 mile), heading NE.

After a few hundred paces the path is improved as a wider farm track joins to the R. For some distance it keeps quite close to the drystone wall on the L and views are possible to the S. These are partially obscured by the slope, but the small lake of Llyn Erddyn to thee sw should be visible in clear weather. After about 500 paces the path leaves the wall to head due E. The rising slope to the L obscures further views in this direction, except for the summit dome of Y Llethr. However, as you continue the views to the S compensate for this. The tiny lake of Llyn Dulyn, just north of Diffwys, is visible near to the natural rocky dam that extends from Y Llethr in the N to Diffwys in the S. This jagged ridge of exposed crags is called Crib-y-rhiw. A short distance further on, the gain in height allows the Llyn Bodlyn reservoir to be viewed to the sw. If the weather is good, you might even be able to spot a few tourists having a picnic by the lakeside. The path continues on, but the gradient will begin to ease as you approach the S end of the summit of Y Llethr. The terrain becomes very wet indeed in this region and you should make your way carefully from one grassy clump to the next to keep your feet dry! This section is only a few metres long and so will not present prolonged inconvenience.

From the marshy section you should head for the corner of the drystone walls ahead, where there is an L-stile. The view over this wall to the E is refreshing and in great contrast to that to the w encountered so far: you look down across short, steep grass slopes in the foreground to the huge expanse of land S of Trawsfynydd. This flat expanse is interrupted by little except the cluster of hills to the SE of Garn Fâch (550m/1,850ft) and Y Garn (620m/2,034ft) and adopts a mixture of deep rusty reds and oranges in the autumn. Continue over the L-stile and up the very steep,

grassy slope ahead, following to the L of the drystone wall. There is another L-stile immediately on the R which should be disregarded, and at the time of writing there was a stack of new L-stiles stored in reserve here. The ensuing steep slope is the s end of Y Llethr's unusual dome-like summit and requires stamina not tested until now. The drystone wall on the R is very tidy and appears new while behind you, looking S, there are intriguing views along Crib-y-rhiw with its small pond and serrated crags. After a few hundred paces the gradient reduces uniformly and the small summit cairn of Y Llethr will come into view. The drystone wall runs right along the summit ridge and provides limited shelter from the mountain breeze. The summit is unusual, being almost free from rocks and covered in smooth, short turf. This provides a comfortable place to rest and look down on Cwm Nantcol, to the w below.

The way to Rhinog Fach   *Allow 1½ hours*

From Y Llethr, the way to Rhinog Fach begins with an easy stroll along the ridge, following the drystone wall to the NE. The path descends very gradually and is clear, keeping close to the wall as it progresses. Quite rapidly the slope to the N gives way to the magnificent views beyond of Rhinog Fach, a huge rugged pile of stone blocks and boulders, with the quiet lake of Llyn Hywel before it. Behind Rhinog Fach, the furrowed w slopes of Rhinog Fawr can be seen across the head of Cwm Nantcol. As you continue the walking remains very easy, although the path becomes more uneven as the craggy N side of Y Llethr exerts a more powerful influence on the terrain. You must keep rigidly to the wall until you see a small cairn very close to the path. This indicates where the best route of descent begins and a noticeable path disappears down the slope. If you miss the cairn you will reach a precipitous edge after a few paes and will be able to view Llyn y Bi to the E. You should retrace your steps and follow the way down from the cairn, since descending elsewhere is both dangerous and difficult.

The path is steep and very eroded, to the extent that it is very clear as a sandy trail down the mountainside. After several hundred paces it flattens out and continues its N route towards Llyn Hywel ahead. The path descends a wide gully in the N face of Y Llethr and consequently becomes sheltered very quickly. It is important to note that the route does not approach close to the lake until it is on the E side of the water, so do not head directly for the shore as you will lose too much height. The correct path strikes off some distance before the lakeside and heads NE over the lumpy crags and hillocks that make up the rim around the lake. The path is clear, but you need to look for it occasionally when it dips out of sight behind large outcrops. When the path flattens it becomes very wet. However, this does not prevail for long, as the path soon meets the wall again to the E of the lake, where the ground is firmer and drier.

The N and E sides of Llyn Hywel are steep and in places complete slabs of bedrock descend into the deep waters. Elsewhere, coarse screes containing large blocks of rock tumble into the lake. The path avoids all these hazards and proceeds amid heather and rocks with the wall a short distance to the R. Llyn y Bi can be viewed to the E, it is shallow and host to expanses of reeds that give it a rusty appearance. To the W the path approaches Llyn Hywel quite closely and continues on a flat course towards the base of Rhinog Fach. At this point (MR 665266) there is a notice on the wall informing you that the path is not a right of way but is on loan to the National Park Authority. It is closed every year on 5 February to retain this status.

As you continue along the path, a high bank develops on the L on which there is a small cairn. The gradient increases rapidly here and starts to test your legs! A path leaves to the L, which should be disregarded as it leads to the lakeside. The recommended path continues to follow the wall on its now inclined heading, due N. The path quickly changes to a terrain of rock chips and small, loose boulders devoid of vegetation which can be slippery, so take care. After a few more paces the terrain deteriorates further as the path enters a small, coarse scree. The path crosses this and remains clear, despite the walking becoming uncomfortable and testing.

Beyond the coarse scree there is a flat plateau with a craggy outcrop to the L. Behind this the block-shaped crags of the SW side of Rhinog Fach can be seen, while the path follows the wall across the flat section to the R of another large scree ahead. The wall forms a sheltered corner a few paces further along and the scree has spilled over, beginning to fill this area. The path traverses the small section of rocks and boulders and quickly enters a gentler region that is dotted with broad patches of heather. Keeping faithfully to the wall, the route changes from its prevailing N direction to just NW and the gradient declines quickly. After about 100 paces you will reach the rather diminutive summit cairn among thick heather, positioned at the end of the drystone wall.

From the summit of Rhinog Fach the dominant feature is the lower stretch of Cwm Nantcol with its green, fertile plain reaching out towards the coast in the W. To the N there is an impressive view of the SW slopes of Rhinog Fawr with their characteristic deep channelling. These deep grooves complicate any attempts to trek across the slopes because of the deep ruts and bulbous clumps of heather. Interrupting the view to the N is a smaller satellite outcrop of Rhinog Fach which is visited next.

The way to Llyn Cwmhosan and back to Cwm Nantcol
Allow 1½ hours

From the summit of Rhinog Fach, proceed NE for the first few hundred paces before returning to the previous N bearing. The path is very clear at this stage since it weaves through heather and boggy peat patches that are susceptible to erosion and footprints. You will quickly lose a few metres in height before reaching a flatter section. Looking behind you to the S, you will notice that the summit of Rhinog Fach adorns a distinctive crag at the S end of a short, uneven ridge, and other walkers standing on the summit may well be silhouetted against the early afternoon sky. The terrain is good at this stage and you will make rapid progress N as the path is clear and rocky through the heather. You will pass a small cairn from which you must continue, disregarding a path to the R that connects a lower-level traverse of the E side of the summit. After only a few hundred paces more you will reach another cairn. At this point (MR 665275) the path turns sharp L to head W, and you must follow: to the N there are steep drops followed by impassable screes.

The change of direction to the W coincides with the beginning of a positive descent. The path winds unpredictably, crossing outcrop and heather, but remains clear and easy to follow. As the descent develops the rocks will become looser. It is important not to become complacent, as the ground gets progressively more difficult and awkward. On the map the path appears to end at ME 662275; at this point it descends a steep section of loose shale to the L of a large outcrop. After this the green, lush valley holding Llyn Cwmhosan (not yet in sight) can be seen, with its spidery network of paths. You are still a considerable distance away from the valley floor and it is important not to rush to get there. You might need to use your hands occasionally to get down steep parts of the route, but there is never any great exposure or associated danger. After the immediate descent the path is absorbed by a lumpy, coarse scree over which you should pick your way carefully. To the N Llyn Cwmhosan comes into view, providing the foreground to a particularly captivating perspective of Rhinog Fawr that will improve further as you continue.

Crossing the scree is tiring and makes calf muscles despair! However, it is over quickly and you will soon join a much better path that heads N. This path is made up of the exposed roots of the abundant surrounding heather and is a great relief after the screes and shale tracks. Unfortunately, it lasts for only a short distance before petering out in favour of crossing a coarse moraine to the L. This channel of large boulders covers a submerged river, which can be heard rushing below. At first it appears daunting, but the rocks are solid and safe and the river far smaller than it appears to the ear.

On the far side of the hidden river a better path is regained, which heads N down the narrow valley towards Llyn Cwmhosan. This path is rocky and

Afternoon reflections of Rhinog Fawr.

uneven, and thick heather encroaches to the L as it follows the L side of the cwm for a few paces. The path will divide 100 paces or so further down the cwm. Here you should fork R to head for Llyn Cwmhosan. This path is clear and crosses the cwm, fording the river via reliable stepping stones. After this the path climbs a sharp incline to get over the rim of the hollow in which the lake is set. In comparison with the earlier descent, the terrain is now very easy and picturesque.

Llyn Cwmhosan is a small lake, no more than 100m (110 yd) long, and appears quite shallow. It is surrounded by spongy marsh grass and reeds which give the impression that approaching the lake is not possible. In reality, if you are careful and follow the numerous sheep tracks around the lakeside, the surrounding ground is reasonably firm and dry and you can get to the water's edge. Fantastic views of Rhinog Fawr can be enjoyed from this position. Llyn Cwmhosan appears to be sourced by small tributaries and natural drainage and, as it is sheltered by the W screes of Rhinog Fach, is usually very still and calm. The shallow waters foster rich vegetation below the surface which gives the lake a variety of colours through the seasons. A final rest here before the concluding stage of the walk is strongly recommended.

From Llyn Cwmhosan, proceed with the lake on your R, heading due N. As before, the path continues to be clear and easy to follow. Within a few paces it descends a small gorge and an L-stile crossing a drystone wall comes into view ahead, further down. The remote tranquillity enhanced by Llyn Cwmhosan continues as you approach the head of Cwm Nantcol and you might hear the Afon Cwmnantcol some distance ahead. When you have crossed the wall via the L-stile you will need to cross the river immediately afterwards, using a few stepping stones. This is followed by a short section of usually very wet ground and more stepping stones, until you reach a wider path. Turn L here (MR 660281) to head SE.

The route now begins the descent of Cwm Nantcol via Bwlch Drws-Ardudwy. The immediate area is a flat plateau of thick heather and marshland, rising to both sides to the Rhinogyll. It is a quiet place and there are few sheep around.

However, it is also rich in wildlife: in the past, the author has stumbled on a rather tired fox, and on another occasion observed an adder dart ahead of his footsteps. The path meanders a fair distance from the wall and the river to the L and is set on a very easy gradient. The marshy ground prevails as you continue and in places the path is supported by slabs to keep the mud at bay. You will soon pass an L-stile far on the L which crosses the wall; this is the path that forked L earlier, before Llyn Cwmhosan, and you should disregard it. The river gurgles its way down the cwm and the path tracks it accurately.

Looking behind you to the NE, the cluster of peaks around Rhinog Fawr develops and makes a fine view. Be sure to take in the scenery, because it changes rapidly as the outcrops ahead obscure the impressive backdrop. This is temporary effect, however, since the lower crags of Rhinog Fach to the S give way to pleasant views of Y Llethr, now a long way away to the S side of Cwm Nantcol.

As you progress down the valley the scenery continues to impress. Another drystone wall will join closely to the L and you will need to cross several brooks by means of small stone footbridges. There are also numerous wet sections forded by stepping stones and small cairns to guide in places where the path has been disguised by the mud and peat. The path continues through two sections of drystone wall; it crosses the first through a gap and the second via a small wrought-iron gate. The path now follows the wall faithfully for several hundred paces. You will start to notice derelict farm buildings on the R and, as you continue, some modern inhabited ones further on. You will need to use an L-stile to cross a gate ahead and will be able to see a narrow tarmac track ahead. The path quickly crosses a stream via stepping stones and joins the tarmac. There is a small clearing on the R which is used for limited parking and the track continues to the R towards the small farmstead of Nantcol. This way should be disregarded in favour of the descending tarmac, heading SW. You should now walk the remaining tranquil steps along the tarmac, past quiet streams and sleepy farms, until you reach the parking space where the route began, 1km (⅝ mile) further on.

Alternative routes

There is a suitable short cut that omits Rhinog Fach from the route but includes much of the remaining features of this walk. As you progress along the E side of Llyn Hywel, as described earlier, you will pass a path that descends to the L heading for the lakeside. Follow this path around the N perimeter of the lake, heading due W. After a few hundred paces it will leave the lake heading NW, to descend a narrow cwm. The path is clear and the descent easier than that recommended earlier via the screes. It keeps to its NW bearing to meet with the original route after about 1km (⅝ mile) close to Llyn Cwmhosan. From this position you should continue as recommended via Cwm Nantcol back to the parking place.

EXTENSIONS

The terrain of the Rhinogyll is difficult and absorbs energy liberally from the fittest of walkers. However, there is a lengthy extention to this route that includes Rhinog Fawr, part of a medieval trading route called the Roman Steps and other interesting features, which is strongly recommended. Ensure that you have enough time and energy before attempting this alternative. You should follow the route as described until you meet the main path at the head of Cwm Nantcol, just beyond the L-stile from Llyn Cwmhosan, at MR 660281. At this junction, turn R to head NE up the valley. The path is slightly inclined for a few hundred paces and passes very close to the large SE crag of Rhinog Fawr on the L. After this it starts to descend, crosses a drystone wall and then divides, where you should fork to the L. The views ahead are dominated by a large area of coniferous forest. The path follows a heading of NNE and eventually meets the forest edge at an L-stile. At the time of writing, this area of woodland had recently been forested and was therefore clear scrubland. You should continue into the forest. The path loses some definition and is obstructed by fallen trees in places, so keep to the recommended bearing wherever possible.

After several hundred paces, the faint path ends in a junction with a more defined, wide gravel forest track. Here you should turn L and then follow the track as it descends gently into the sheltering forest, heading NW. This section lasts for about 300m (325 yd) before reaching a noticeable clearing and a T-junction. At this point (MR 670298) there is a pretty waterfall a few hundred paces to the R (due E). Known as Pistyll Gwyn, this fall of a few metres height cascades into a deep and narrow plunge pool that is sheltered by thick woodland to all sides and is well worth a visit. To continue the route, however, turn L at the T-junction and head due W. After a few hundred paces, the path leaves the forest via an L-stile where good views of Rhinog Fawr are possible, with the path climbing rapidly into the deep cwm to the R.

The path is clear and narrow and winds gradually up into the mountains, following the route known as the Roman Steps. This once formed a crucial medieval trading route between the W coast of mid-Wales and the E. The path is supported by slabs of stone for much of the way and, although steep, the terrain is not difficult.

To complete the route you should leave the ascent just before it reaches its highest point and becomes enclosed in a narrow gully. A clear path forks L very sharply, partially doubling back on your previous steps, heading SE. This path traverses around the large crag just above the Roman Steps and leads to a small lake called Llyn Du. If you are feeling particularly fit it is possible to reach the summit of Rhinog Fawr quickly from this position (MR 656295). This can be done by scrambling up the zigzag path that heads SW from the S side of the lake, but is only advisable for the more experienced walkers. To continue the extension, you will need to return to the lake and head due W via the path that leaves from the N edge of the water. The ground becomes very difficult here as the path follows the route of a drystone wall, heading WSW, to meet a clear path just S of the eerie lake Gloyw Llyn. The terrain of this section necessitates the regular use of the compass and some improvised route finding. Follow this path due S to meet the tarmac road in Cwm Nantcol after a couple of kilometres. Follow the tarmac track back down the cwm to the layby to complete this mammoth extension to a superb route!

Route 12: CRAIG CAU AND CADAIR IDRIS

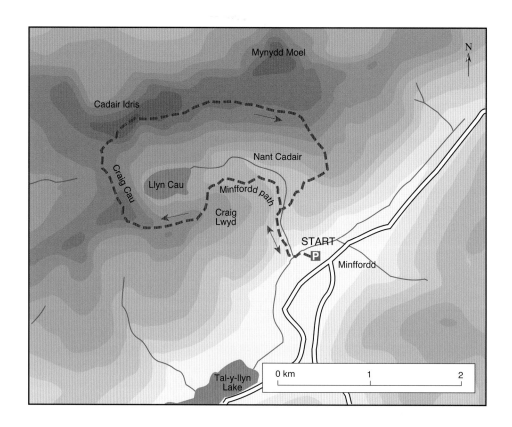

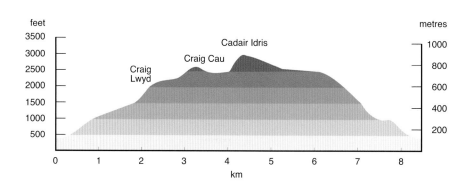

Route 12 • Craig Cau and Cadair Idris

STARTING LOCATION
Minffordd car park.
OLM 23/MR 733116.
Capacity for 40 cars.
Public toilets (may be closed in winter).
Public telephone nearby.

ALTERNATIVE STARTING LOCATION
None.

PUBLIC TRANSPORT
Bus route Dolgellau–Tywyn (no Sunday service)
(along the A487(T) road).

OVERVIEW/INTEREST
Explores an idyllic forest in the S region of the
    Snowdonia National Park.
Visits the extensive Cadair Idris massif and the
    mountain lake of Llyn Cau.
Sheer cliffs and craggy terrain, offering splendid
    views of the Rhinog range and Barmouth Bay.

FOOTPATHS
Paths are very clear throughout.
Higher sections pass areas of some exposure
    where care is required.
Compass is essential for the later sections of the
    route.

GRADING   Moderate
TIME ALLOWANCE   5 hours
DISTANCE
Excluding height   9.25km (5.8 miles)
TOTAL HEIGHT GAINED   974m (3,195ft)
PRINCIPAL HEIGHTS
Craig Cau 791m (2,595ft)
Cadair Idris 893m (2,930ft)

The way to Craig Cau   *Allow 2½ hours*

At the far L corner of the car park, heading NW, there is a signpost denoting the beginning of the Minffordd Path. Follow this wide dirt track, which rapidly becomes a delightful avenue of horse chestnut trees. The path is accompanied by a stream for about 100 paces, which it eventually crosses via a low bridge. Bear L through a wide gate and continue as the path meanders out of the trees and away from the stream. The path is lined with gravel at this stage and subsequently passes through a K-gate. Directly ahead is a rather unusual square house; continue to the L of this, disregarding the minor path which leads into the forest to the R. Further on, the route passes a derelict building on the L and the sound of a river can be heard ahead. The path crosses this river, the Nant Cadair, via a low, wide footbridge and bends to the R towards a small gate. This forms an entrance to the Cadair Idris Nature Reserve, as a plaque here indicates.

The gradient of the route increases rapidly and the path climbs to the N, up into a dense wood of oak trees. This wood was featured in the 1950s film *The Inn of the Sixth Happiness*, which starred Ingrid Bergman. The popularity of this walk is evident from the steps that have been built to reduce the erosion of the path, which continue for much of the forest section. The shelter provided by the trees makes this a tranquil and secluded section of this walk. After about 400 paces the trees give way to boulders and the steps cease. The path then proceeds through open terrain once again and gradually leaves the company of the river. The few oak trees present are soon replaed by silver birch. The route continues to the N, crossing several tributaries, and climbs towards the open moorland visible ahead. Waterfalls to the right can now be seen (and heard!) as the path narrows and passes through a small gate. At this stage, a good view of Mynydd Rugog can be seen to the S in good weather, in between both coniferous and deciduous groups of trees. This hill is a vast, smooth slope covered in dense vegetation.

The gradient relents as the route progresses and the path enters gently inclined moorland, which is peppered with rocky outcrops and boulders. The path descends slightly and almost meets the river known as Nant Cadair. Disregard the lesser path to the R which crosses the river, and continue due N. About 50 paces beyond the river there is a pleasant coniferous wood upon a short natural lawn. Further ahead, the lower slopes of Mynydd Moel can be seen, haphazardly criss-crossed by ancient drystone walls. The route is reasonably flat for the next 500 paces or so and provides an opportunity to view the valley ahead as it gradually opens up. This can be a lush combination of oranges, greens and dramatic greys in the autumn, with the long peak of Mynydd Moel located due N.

The path is easy to follow as it is well trodden, and presently it turns to the W as it circles Craig Lwyd to the L. There are some delightful weatherbeaten trees along the path here, some of which are clinging desperately to the sides of the path as a result of erosion and the effect of the river's course. The route gradually becomes steeper and rockier and Craig Cau looms impressively into view to the W. Craig Cau is the most dramatic peak of the Cadair Idris massif. Indeed, to the newcomer it is easy to mistake it for the Cadair Idris summit, either from the valley or from the peak itself. Adorned with sheer slopes on its N and W sides, it was carved by a glacier in the last ice age, which also left the deep cwm that Llyn Cau now occupies.

After about 500 paces the route winds easily up the S side of this cwm and then meets a large cairn, where it divides (MR 721124). Disregard the R fork (which leads to Llyn Cau) and take the steeper path to the L. As the route progresses the rim of the cwm is reached and Llyn Cau can be seen far below to the R. The glacial erosion that formed the surrounding dramatic landscape is evident everywhere; particularly to the E of the lake a large slab of granite is visible which is scored with striations from these powerful processes. Llyn Cau is a deep azure lake complemented dramatically by the grey flanks of Craig Cau.

As the path continues to climb, it becomes less stable and bends gradually to the R, due W. Looking down the slopes of Mynydd Pentre to the S it is possible to see Llyn Mwyngil (Tal-y-llyn lake), a deep blue-grey expanse of water, with Mynydd Rugog beyond. Cairns are present at regular intervals on the route and are particularly helpful in poor visibility, as the N side of the cwm becomes increasingly exposed. This small ridge is quite wide and is decorated with heather and exposed quartz. As the route progresses the gradient reduces, and views of Llyn Cau become obscured by outcrops of granite to the R. It is unwise to deviate from the path in order to view the lake, since Llyn Cau is

Autumn colours near Craig Cau.

now about 200m (656ft) below and the N sides of Craig Cau are mainly sheer cliffs. In poor visibility, be particularly sure of your compass. The Minffordd Path turns to the NNW for the final few hundred paces to the Craig Cau summit.

Though still uphill, the route becomes relatively easy and a reasonably wide plateau develops, with the summit of Craig Cau visible directly ahead (NNW). The path wanders inwards from the cliff edge, and the wide saddle of Craig Cwm Amarch, which stretches down from the summit, can be seen to the W. The path consists of short grass and rocks and is well trodden. It descends slightly, before rising gently to the precipitous summit of Craig Cau, which is denoted by a large cairn. From Craig Cau, the summit of Cadair Idris can be seen directly to the N, with the grassy S side of Cyfrwy (also known as The Saddle) visible to the NW. To the NE the way to Mynydd Moel can be seen along the Cadair Idris massif, and a pleasant view of the valley formed by the combination of Cadair Idris and Craig Cau is also possible in good weather. To the SW the broad slopes of Mynydd Pencoed appear, and further afield the Llanfihangel region of fields and meadows is visible in the distance. In contrast to the rocky, austere landscape of Cadair Idris, this area is gentle, floral and flat by comparison.

The way to Cadair Idris and back to the Minffordd Path
Allow 2½ hours

From Craig Cau, the way to the summit of Cadair Idris is exhilarating and exposed, frequently interspersed with sheer gullies that afford views of Llyn Cau some 300m (984ft) below. From the Craig Cau summit, the path heads NNW, and passes over an L-stile before descending steeply to the N of Craig Cwm Amarch. At the lowest point a very steep path leaves the ridge to the R and descends rapidly to the lake below, heading E. Disregard this route and continue along the ridge to the N; the correct path rises gradually and becomes more grassy, moving away from the edge of the ridge and hence becoming less exposed. A grassy plain about 20m (22 yd) wide develops to the R and the path gradually changes direction to head NE. The

frequency of cairns diminishes, but the path is well trodden and is easy to follow in all weathers as the risk of exposed cliffs is reduced.

At this stage spectacular views of the N side of Craig Cau can be seen to the rear, looking SE. The sheer gullies from which you viewed Llyn Cau can now be seen, with the barren black cliffs plummeting towards the lake. Small cairns litter the path as the gradual climb steepens and becomes more rocky, with a large boulder scree imposing to the R. After a further 50 paces or so, the summit of Cadair Idris appears ahead. The surrounding views to the valley below are partially obscured as the ridge levels out into a reasonably wide plain, about 20 paces across.

The summit of Cadair Idris is raw and composed of large, loose boulders, not unlike that of Scafell Pike in the Lake District. The large cairn supports a triangulation point, to the W of which is a large hut that provides refuge for those unfortunate enough to be delayed by bad weather. In fine weather, the summit provides rewarding views in all directions. To the W, in the immediate foreground the dramatic cliffs of Cyfry – an attraction for intrepid climbers – can be seen surrounding the lake of Llyn y Gadair. This ridge provides an alternative route for Cadair Idris, known as the Pony Path, which originates from the small settlement of Llanfihangel-y-pennant which lies to the SW. Beyond Cyfry, the seaside resort of Barmouth, with its distinctive rail bridge spanning the neck of the bay, can be seen. To the N, beyond the town of Dolgellau the large, heavy shapes of the Rhinog mountains are visible. In contrast to this range of rather smooth peaks, the S panorama from the Cadair Idris summit is dominated by Craig Cau and the jagged ridge which leads to it, while the E vista is that of Mynydd Moel, the easternmost peak of the Cadair Idris massif.

The route now progresses towards the E; a compass bearing is essential in poor weather, as the summit is wide and can confuse. It is important that the ridge to the E is followed for about 2km (1¼ miles) before the steeper descent is attempted, as the sheer cliffs and screes that constitute the S side of Cadair Idris are potentially dangerous. There are, in fact, two paths available which traverse the ridge. The most N heads off NE from the summit and is recommended as an extension, described below. The more S alternative heads off due E from the summit of Cadair Idris and descends gradually, following the S cliff-tops. On this route, take care not to lose too much height too quickly or deviate from the correct path, which is clear and of well-trodden short, weathered grass. This path traverses through thick heather for 2km (1¼ miles), gradually changing course to the S, before reaching an L-stile which crosses a fence. The ground undulates unpredictably and retains much of its height for a considerable distance. After the L-stile, follow the path, which now continues to the S and descends more rapidly than before. It is also much rockier, with more loose rock, so take care and do not rush. After about 300m (325yd) another L-stile to the R re-crosses the fence. This position (MR 732125) is a particularly good viewpoint for both Craig Cau and Cadair Idris, and is consequently a suitable place for a well-earned break. Looking due W, Craig Cau rises ominously at the head of the valley, while slightly to the N of this the summit of Cadair Idris can be seen.

Continue over the L-stile; the path now meanders passively down towards the small, dense, coniferous forest at the foot of the slope. This path is of lush grass mingling with drystone walls and isolated trees. The descent is gradual and can be quite wet. Follow the path as far as possible, and after a few hundred paces it will meet with the Nant Cadair. Cross the river by means of a group of substantial stepping stones, after which the path almost immediately meets the Minffordd Path that formed the earlier route of ascent. From this position (MR 728121) retrace your steps down through the forest of silver birch and oak to return to the Minffordd car park.

Alternative routes

ESCAPES
You can return earlier by retracing your steps. Otherwise there are no escape routes.

Mynydd Moel on the ascent of Cadair Idris.

EXTENSIONS
It is possible to extend this walk by following the NW path, instead of the S route, from the summit of Cadair Idris. This allows you to take in three extra summits along the ridge, including Mynydd Moel (863m/2,832ft). It also prolongs your appreciation

of the views to the N and enables you to view the small lake, Llyn Gafr, which lies in this direction. The route goes over an L-stile just before the summit of Mynydd Móel, which is marked by a large, wide cairn. From the summit, continue in a SE direction. Keep the cwm of Llyn Cau in view to the right. The path is a little indistinct, but follows a fence closely for most of the descent from here. After about 700m (760yd), the S path from Cadair Idris joins this route to the R via an L-stile, thereby returning you to the main route of descent already described.

Route 13: CADAIR BERWYN, MOEL SYCH
AND THE SEVENTH WONDER

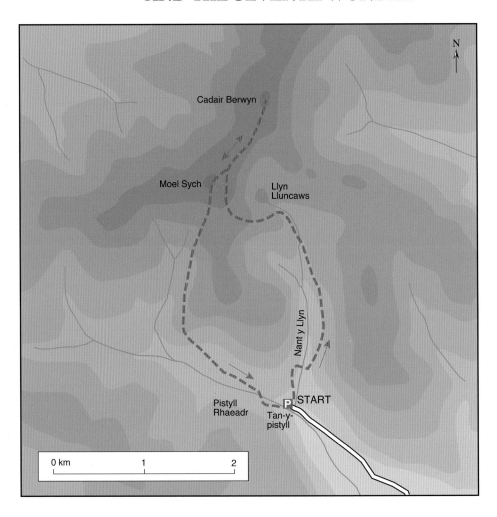

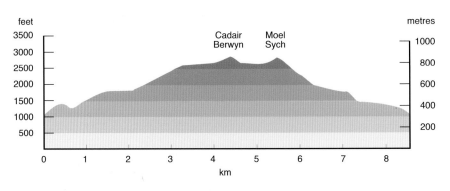

Route 13 • Cadair Berwyn, Moel Sych and the Seventh Wonder

STARTING LOCATION
Pistyll Rhaeadr car park at Tan-y-pistyll (small charge).
OSLR 125/MR 074295.
Capacity for 25 cars, with limited free parking available nearby on the side of the lane.
Public toilets.

ALTERNATIVE STARTING LOCATION
None.

PUBLIC TRANSPORT
None.

OVERVIEW/INTEREST
Explores a beautiful valley in the Berwyn range.
Easy climbs to Cadair Berwyn and Moel Sych peaks.
Relaxing and very enjoyable ridge walking.
Concludes at the stunning Pistyll Rhaeadr waterfalls, known as the Seventh Wonder of Wales.

FOOTPATHS
Route is not a right of way, but is permitted for use by the landowner.
Paths are unclear in places, but route-finding is not difficult.
Compass is useful in poor visibility.
Sections of the route can be boggy and wet.

GRADING Easy
TIME ALLOWANCE 4 hours
DISTANCE
Excluding height 9km (5.6miles)
TOTAL HEIGHT GAINED 827m (2,713ft)
PRINCIPAL HEIGHTS
Cadair Berwyn 827m (2,713ft)
Moel Sych 827m (2,713ft)

The way to Cadair Berwyn   *Allow 2 hours*

Leave the car park at Tan-y-pistyll via its entrance and walk a short distance down the narrow tarmac approach road, heading E. Pass through a small gate on the L side of the road, and follow the path as it skirts to the R of a small copse. After a short distance it crosses a drystone wall via an L-stile and splits into two. The path to the L is waymarked by yellow arrows and is the tourist path to the head of the Pistyll Rhaeadr waterfall. Disregard this and take the R fork, which continues passing through a slight landslip of slate debris. As the route progresses, the valley of the river Nant y Llyn falls away to the R and the path clings to the L side, affording pleasant views of the lower slopes of the Berwyns. After only a few paces a tangled mass of sheep paths descends the steep slope to the R to the banks of the Nant y Llyn; once again, this path should be ignored. The correct route follows a wide, more established track up a steady incline, now heading due N.

After a few hundred paces of steady climbing, the track reaches a subtle crossroads on almost the same level as the river, which lies to the R down a shallow descent. Turn R here and head for the river, which is easily crossed by means of some makeshift stepping stones. The path then crosses a rusty, unhinged metal gate and heads SE as it climbs the bank opposite; it effectively zigzags in order to cross the river and is heading for the long, straight path that ascends the W side of the valley of the Nant y Llyn. This path can be seen clearly from the river, heading off into the distance. On climbing from the river you will meet it abruptly and should turn L, to head N once more.

The following section of the route is very pleasant indeed. It climbs gradually and effortlessly, rising quickly above the valley floor where a number of sheep pens can be seen below to the L, these resembling a small maze of drystone walls.

Deep mid-winter in the Berwyns.

Meanwhile, the impressive massif of Moel Sych (rounded s end) and Cadair Berwyn (jagged N peak) comes into view and dominates the panorama to the N. There are several P-stiles that are perfectly placed for resting and taking in the scenery as you continue N. However, do not forsake the views to the s: the small valley of the Nant y Llyn meets with the larger valley of the Afon Rhaeadr, and there is a confusion of steep spurs and forested slopes near to the falls of Pistyll Rhaeadr.

As you progress the path remains clear and firm, but the valley rises to meet it and there are some steep crags to the R. In this area the river is joined by several small tributaries and it shrinks rapidly as you climb further up the valley. The path continues N, but tends slightly to the w as it approaches some high ground on the L; there is also a wooden waymarking stump near here indicating that the path is permitted and is not a public right of way. Soon after this the path heads NW, but remains clear and crosses a small stream by means of stepping stones. A large peat shelf develops to the L and the path skirts around it, following the stream which lies to the R. Soon excellent views are possible across the circular lake of Llyn Lluncaws, which lies at the foot of Moel Sych, to Cadair Berwyn in the N. Although the path is reasonably flat in this area it will soon begin the steep climb from the lake, up the sweeping s spur of Moel Sych and on to the Berwyn ridge. Be sure to disregard any smaller paths that head off N for Cadair Berwyn: you should be walking due w with Llyn Lluncaws on the R.

The route now becomes quite steep and more rocky than before, as the thick heather gives way to short grass and thin topsoil. As the climb progresses it becomes more exposed. Keep to the path and walk away from the edge wherever possible. This route clings to the lip of the cwm and consequently circles the small lake, presenting some fine views of it and the gentle landscape beyond, to the E. However, in winter it is advisable to keep well away from the edge of the cwm, as the snow tends to drift around boulders and small landslips to make the surrounding slopes treacherous. The gradient then reduces and the terrain becomes easier as the summit ridge is reached. Here you can reward yourself with a break if necessary. To the L you will see a cluster of L-stiles, which should be disregarded at present. Continue on NE along the ridge, which is relatively wide and grassy, towards the summit of Cadair Berwyn. Ahead you will see the rocky outcrop which forms a false summit; you will need to cross a drystone wall via an L-stile just short of this, following which the ground is noticeably more rocky. The true summit of Cadair Berwyn lies beyond this outcrop and is marked by a triangulation point. It is an easy stroll to conquer from the false summit!

Cadair Berwyn is 827m (2,713ft) high and is the highest N point of a precipitous ridge of which Moel Sych is the S end. Visible from the summit are the rolling hillsides leading to the small village of Llanarmon Mynydd-mawr to the E, Cadair Bronwen (formerly Cadair Ffronwen) to the N, and the smooth slopes that surround Llandrillo to the W. The ridge is especially rewarding as it has not been subject to extensive erosion by either weather or walker, and is therefore very satisfying to both the feet and the eyes!

The way to Moel Sych and Pistyll Rhaeadr Falls
Allow 2 hours

From the summit of Cadair Berwyn, retrace your steps back towards the false summit. It is important to keep close to the fence on the R, as before long the way leaves the previous route of ascent and proceeds in the direction of the summit of Moel Sych to the SW. The path crosses an adjoining fence via an L-stile and the summit cairn of Moel Sych, at 827m (2,713ft), lies only a little way beyond. Near to the cairn is another L-stile, via which the ridge path continues in the direction of Milltir Gerrig to the W. Disregard this route and continue by following the path which rolls gently down the slopes to the S, close to the fence crossed previously. The route is no longer demanding and requires little effort, especially since the thick grass and heather cushion your steps.

As the descent develops, very picturesque views unfold ahead of the Rhaeadr valley and, beyond this, the Tanat valley, which guides the eye towards Shrewsbury far away to the SE. The slope eases near an L-stile via which you cross the guiding fence. After a short distance the terrain changes, becoming more rocky and enclosed. The path joins a tarmac track and you should turn R along this, leaving again almost immediately when another path forks to the L towards an L-stile. Having crossed the drystone wall via this stile, continue into the very pretty copse beyond. From this

position Pistyll Rhaeadr Falls should be clearly audible, and presents a refreshing and unusual guide! This route leads to the top of the falls and extreme care is needed, especially with small children, who should be held firmly by the hand, as the falls are some 80m (262ft) high and there is no fence or similar barrier.

Pistyll Rhaeadr Falls are known as the Seventh Wonder of Wales, a title justly deserved as they are unspoilt and provide much aesthetic pleasure. Despite their popularity, they are deeply hidden in the surrounding tall evergreen trees, which adds to their allure. There are various short routes from the head of the falls to the bottom. These are well worn through use and are very steep and wet in places. The car park, and the small teashop at Tan-y-Pistyll, are only a small stroll from the foot of Pistyll Rhaeadr Falls.

Alternative routes

ESCAPES
This route is not demanding, and there are no escape routes other than simply turning around and retracing your steps to Pistyll Rhaeadr prior to the final ascent of Cadair Berwyn. After this is is best to persevere and complete the walk, as this is the shortest option.

EXTENSIONS
There are two delightful extensions to this walk. You might like to continue along the ridge from Cadair Berwyn to the N. This leads to the twin peak of Cadair Bronwyn, the associated spurs, Bwrdd Arthur and Bwlch Maen Gwynedd, and passes the smaller peak of Tomle (741m/2,431ft) to the E. From Cadair Bronwyn it is best to retrace your steps to Cadair Berwyn and continue the route as already described.

The second extension takes you SW from the summit of Moel Sych instead of due S, as in the recommended route. This follows a steeper descent, via Cwm-Rhiwiau, and passes prehistoric sites of interest, including a stone circle and a stone row. From these, follow the path SE, which leads to the head of Pistyll Rhaeadr Falls, as already described.

Route 14: CWM CYWARCH AND THE ARAN

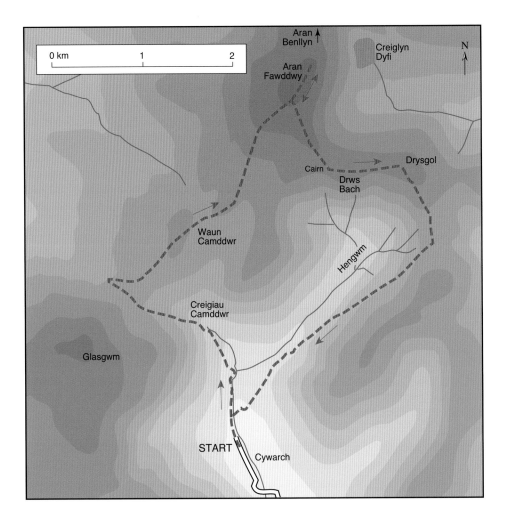

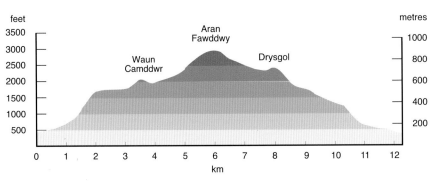

Route 14 • Cwm Cywarch and the Aran

STARTING LOCATION
Cwm Cywarch.
OLM 23/MR 854185.
Car parking capacity for 10 cars.
Public toilet.

ALTERNATIVE STARTING LOCATION
None.

PUBLIC TRANSPORT
None.

OVERVIEW/INTEREST
Explores an exquisite valley, with views of Craig
   Cywarch.
Gentle ridge walking and a scenic ascent of Aran
   Fawddwy.
Visits the RAF memorial and then descends via
   the long, beautiful valley of Hengwm.

FOOTPATHS
Paths are clear throughout.
Expansive ridge requires the use of a compass.
Very wet and boggy in places.
Waymarked for much of the route.

GRADING   Moderate
TIME ALLOWANCE   5½ hours
DISTANCE
Excluding height   12.25km (7.7miles)
TOTAL HEIGHT GAINED   920m (3,018ft)
PRINCIPAL HEIGHTS
Aran Fawddwy 905m (2,970ft)
Aran Benllyn 885m (2,905ft)
Drysgol 745m (2,445ft)

The way to Aran Fawddwy   *Allow 3 hours*

The mountains known as the Aran – Aran
Fawddwy and Aran Benllyn – are the two highest
points on a ridge that is approximately 8km
(5 miles) long. It stretches from Bala in the N almost
to Dinas Mawddwy in the S. The Aran are isolated
from the N because of the considerable distance
from Bala to the range. The same is true from Dinas
Mawddwy, except that a narrow tarmac road serves
the walker well for the latter. This tarmac road
weaves gently down a wide U-shaped valley called
Cwm Cywarch, and it is not until you are within a
couple of kilometres of the mountains that it is
possible to see the distinctive crags at the head of
Cwm Cywarch, below Glasgwm, that make the
journey so very worthwhile. In comparison with N
Snowdonia, this inaccessibility has discouraged the
less determined tourists, even though the scenery
and walking are in many ways superlative.

At the head of Cwm Cywarch, where the road
is degraded from yellow to white on the map, there
is a large flat area that provides room for about ten
vehicles. You will need to park both carefully and
considerately, as wet conditions could complicate
this arrangement. The area is not an official car
park, is not marked on the map, and the resident
farmer may request that you park in a more
suitable place if necessary. There is a single Portaloo
across the road near a fence, while the nearest
public telephone is a traditional red box about
0.5km (⅓ mile) back along the road towards Dinas
Mawddwy.

From the grassy parking area, walk along the
tarmac track in a N direction. Almost immediately,
you will enter a narrow section of the track
enclosed on either side by fences and a few
deciduous trees such as sycamores, mountain ash
and hawthorn. In summer there are buttercups
along the grass verges, and foxgloves cling to the
base of the fences and their stone supports. After
about 100 paces on this flat track you will pass a
wide aluminium gate on your L and then notice a
stream crossed by a ford and footbridge on your R.
There is also a yellow waymarking arrow pointing
in the direction of the bridge with the wording
'Aran Fawddwy'. This forms the return route and
should be disregarded for now. A few paces further

on you will pass a path leaving to the L, which should also be ignored. This is shortly followed by another metal gate, also on the L. After this you should pass through a gate across the tarmac track and continue for a few paces until you reach two more gates separated by a K-gate. The metal gate leads to the farm and this should be disregarded; use the K-gate, which allows you to pass around the farm buildings without intruding and disturbing the residents. At this stage there are still several deciduous trees nearby, attracted by the stream which runs close by on the R. Around the farm the route is waymarked efficiently, first L and then R, which also has the words 'Llwybr' and 'Footpath' on a piece of slate hung on a drystone wall to your L. As the path now leaves the company of both the farm buildings and the river, the trees thin out and the ground becomes more rocky and barren. There are occasional clumps of reeds and a wire fence replaces the stream to the R. You should also notice a gradual increase in gradient as the path proceeds. It subsequently turns slightly to the E and approaches a wooden gate and L-stile. Use the latter, as the gate is rickety and difficult to close.

To the W you will now see the craggy E slopes of Glasgwm, the summit presently hidden from view by these crags. They are surprisingly large for this relatively unknown area and have a wild presence. The S extent of the crags is known as Craig Cywarch, while the N end turns gracefully to the W, marking the recommended route ahead of you. To the E are the large, grassy slopes of Waun Goch that form the symmetrical valley of Hengwm; this is adorned by the ridge-peak of Drysgol at the NE end, with Pen Main in front of it. It is the combination of these features which currently hides both Aran Fawddwy and Aran Benllyn from view. You will pass a rusty gate on the L, but the path continues towards a rather tall L-stile only 50 paces or so after the previous one. Take care with this stile, as it crosses a high drystone wall and is followed by a patch of nettles! There is a hole in the wall for sheep to scuttle through when walkers disturb their grazing. To the left, just after the tall stile, there is a useful route guide. It is framed from the elements and you can check your position on this chart if necessary. Continue on for a further

The natural beauty of Cwm Cywarch.

50 paces or so until a smaller path leaves to the L which is waymarked three times over, firstly by distinctive yellow arrows and then also for 'Rhyrdrymain' and 'Aran'.

The gradient increases considerably on this path and, although narrow, it is distinct and clear due to the furrow it follows through the surrounding ferns and assorted vegetation. Far to your R you will be able to see some disused mine workings and the associated buildings, while up ahead you should be able to spot the forthcoming L-stile, about 25 paces distant. In this area the foxgloves seem to have

taken a stronghold across the hillside and they stand out, bright pink, in late June. The waymarking continues and makes this walk relaxing, with few worries about navigation at this stage. There are not many trees on this part of the walk, which makes conspicuous the two large sycamores ahead and the large, ugly dead one which stands just before them on the L. These trees denote the point where the path enters into deeper vegetation, and you may well be able to smell the light scent of the ferns that now enclose both you and the path. Look behind you at Cwm Cywarch, stretching SE rowards Dinas Mawddwy: this valley is not unlike the Tanat valley that leads to the Berwyn range in the NE.

The path which runs among the ferns is of short grass and can be wet and slippery. The ferns tend to attract insects – generally cowflies that have a nasty bite – but these are soon defeated by the breeze that strengthens as you climb. Hence there is some incentive to grit your teeth and move fast! High above you to the L are the tall gullies of Craig Cywarch. The path is now waymarked by faded yellow arrows painted occasionally on rocks.

As the path turns gradually to the W, the head of the cwm will come into view for the first time. It is made up of a pleasant combination of lush grass and scattered rocks and boulders; opposite is a group of staggered waterfalls, to the L of

Creigiau Camddwr. You should be able to hear the river below, collectively known as the Camddwr, but the path rises high above it now so the sight of it may be obscured. There is a sizeable landslip on the R and the path clings desperately to the side here, to become firm once more a few paces further on, where more waymarking arrows will be seen on the rocks. These arrows are eventually followed by a post that points you in the direction of a wide footbridge. Follow this signing down a short bank to the bridge, which is wide and has a handrail on the R. This crosses the river so that you are now to the N of it. The path changes appearance on this side of the river and becomes more rocky, narrower and unpredictable in its ascent of Cwm Cywarch. It is reinforced with shale in places where landslips have done their worst. After about 50 paces you will pass another large sycamore on the L, followed by a large boulder on the same side. The path then meanders haphazardly up the hillside and you need to be more vigilant than previously, although the route is not complex as you should be heading for the top of the cwm to the WNW. The path follows the river to within a few paces, so you should meet up with it easily if you lose track at any stage. Further on there is a large boulder to the L that is positioned to provide excellent shelter from the merciless midday sun or an icy wind. It is a perfect place for a break and a look around at the smooth slopes of Hengwm to the E and Pen Main slightly further to the N.

As is often found on these rugged Welsh peaks (compare, for example, the latter stages of the ascent of the Watkin Path on Route 4), the path deteriorates as small screes intrude and it has to zigzag its way over the best route of ascent. Here it may be necessary to use your hands in a few places as the path climbs high above the river. This section does not last long, however, and you will soon cross a small tributary to the river below. The screes break up and allow wild daisies and buttercups to replace them – much better! After a further 50 paces or so the path flattens out considerably and passes a small waterfall to your L. This cascades down into a small chasm, and there is also a great deal of vegetation clambering out around the deep

hole. There is a small fence on the L and the path is made up predominantly of short grass that makes walking very enjoyable at this stage. The path continues quite close to the rusty wire fence, and after about 100 paces passes a derelict farm building on the L.

As the path over the wide saddle between Glasgwm and Aran Fawddwy continues, the ground gets progressively wetter and more spongy, and there is also more evidence of a peat soil-base. As on the previous sections of the route, there are still occasional yellow arrows painted on stones to guide you and these should keep you to a bearing of NW. In good visibility you should see a large, upright boulder on the horizon, about 100 paces distant. This also has an arrow on it pointing NW and is valuable in poor visibility. You are now at the highest point of the saddle between Glasgwm and Aran Fawddwy and the latter can be seen clearly to the NE as a shallow cone about 2km (1¼ miles) away. The intermediate expanse of waterlogged moorland can be treacherous and is not to be investigated without respect for the path and a compass. There are large peat bogs and shallow ponds throughout the gradual climb to the summit of Aran Fawddwy and only in the height of summer is the land ever safe enough to be lost in. The upright boulder indicates that a few paces beyond it the moorland path that crosses to the Aran begins. It is well waymarked by a combination of 'Y Aran' and 'No dogs'. Just beyond these signs there is a large peat bog which the path crosses deftly, changing direction from NW to head due E for the first few hundred paces. It will immediately be evident that the ground ahead is extremely wet, as the path is reinforced by horizontal fence posts woven together into a robust matting. This distributes your weight and makes the walking very easy. You are now on the brown path on the map that leaves the green path after the ascent of Cwm Cywarch at MR 839202, the position of the upright boulder. Please note that this is a permitted path as opposed to a public right of way.

The path along the saddle is waymarked by white-tipped posts, and these will lead you to the L of a small boggy lake which is spiked by reeds across its surface. After about 50 paces you will pass two L stiles arranged at right angles to each other on your L. These should be disregarded in favour of the path, which continues on a straight course to the NE, towards Aran Fawddwy in the distance. As the route progresses, additional peaks will come into view on your L. On more N bearings than Rhobell Fawr are the Arenigs, incorporating the characteristic cone shape of Arenig Fawr. On more w bearings are the ugly, almost lumpy peaks of the Rhinogyll.

The ground beneath your feet gets progressively wetter until the land is awash with reeds and sodden peat. Fortunately, long planks of wood have been laid to provide dry walking across this large area of marsh and these continue for several hundred metres. A wire fence is also present to the L, and this serves as an additional guide for much of the forthcoming route of ascent. There are a few reasonably large outcrops of rock to the L as well. After 1km (⅝ mile) on this path you will approach two L-stiles about 20 paces apart, which cross a fence that proceeds E–w across the saddle. On the map the path is shown to cross at least one of these stiles, but in reality a clear path is evident leading to the R, keeping the fence on its L and so disregarding the L-stiles altogether. This path continues with the fence to its L for the next 1km (⅝ mile) and is recommended, as it is dry and clear. It climbs gradually to the NE and passes a concentration of L-stiles, which should also be disregarded. About 100 paces beyond these L-stiles you will pass a large rock outcrop to the L and the path, together with companion fence, will change directly slightly to continue on a bearing of NNE, to the left of the summit – which does not seem to get much closer! Do not forget to keep looking behind you, because the view is constantly developing: to the sw the characteristic long, midpointed shape of Cadair Idris can be seen if the mist or haze allows.

There are at least four aircraft crash sites on the Aran, one of which is hidden in a steep gully to the N of the summit of Aran Fawddwy, with many of the heavier pieces of wreckage now lying around the lake of Creiglyn Dyfi. The other sites are scattered widely around the s side of the summit, and as you continue to follow the path near the fence you may come across the odd piece of fuselage. These bits of wreckage are usually devoid of paint and are fragile enough to be rattled by the mountain breeze. As you progress, the path gets steeper as it approaches the last part of the ascent. You will eventually see several signposts worded 'Cwm cywarch' heading in the reverse direction. The ground is much more rocky and the fence has deteriorated by this stage; long pieces of loose, rusty wire from it fall across the path, so be careful not to trip on them. You will pass an L-stile to the L which should be disregarded, and a few paces further on you should be able to see a distinctive boulder that is half white, half granite. From a distance this appears to have been painted, but in fact it is half made up of very pure quartz. Just beyond this boulder is another L-stile over the fence to the L, which you should also ignore. You are now close to the fence on your L, with what appears to be the summit of Aran Fawddwy rising sharply to the right at MR 858220. Do not be tempted to venture E to climb away from the fence, as this rise is a false summit and the real thing is still several hundred paces NE. However, if you want to rest the false summit is ideal and there is a large cairn to provide some shelter. It also affords a good view of the summit of Aran Fawddwy, which can be distinguished since its triangulation point is clearly visible ahead.

The most direct route to the summit is to keep next to the fence until it is necessary to cross it via an L-stile. There is now very little vegetation around the path, with the surrounding area consisting of rock chippings and dust. After the stile you are free from the guidance of the fence for the first time in about 3km (1¾ miles) and its role is subsequently adopted by a trail of small cairns. These might be hidden by snow in winter, but the summit is clearly visible ahead. At the time of writing there was a pile of new fence posts on the R just before the final climb up to the triangulation point. This is an easy clamber over small, loose rocks, with the summit right at the edge of the E precipice. This is very exposed and, although it is possible to view the lake of Creiglyn Dyfi if you venture to the edge, it is strongly recommended

that you go no further. The cliffs of the E face of Aran Fawddwy are virtually sheer and almost 300m (984ft) in height. Children should be restrained at all times while on the summit.

There are many pleasant views from here. The W panorama is now dominated by the long, wide saddle that you crossed from the foot of Glasgwm. Known as Waun Camddwr, this resembles an expansive, undulating green carpet. In the background are Cadair Idris, the Rhinogs and the Arenigs. You will be fortunate if the weather is good enough to render these peaks visible in detail, since the winter mist or summer haze can obscure them to the point where they are merely faint blue shapes. The green carpet stretching to Glasgwm is speckled with peat bogs and is neatly tucked into the valleys of Hengwm in the foreground and Cwm Cywarch beyond, while in-between these is the grassy rise of Pen Main. The immense spur in front of Hengwm is that of Drysgol, which is explored shortly. To the W the beautiful panorama of mid-Wales continues. There are comparatively few 'famous' peaks in this direction, but this does not detract from the pleasant view of the land surrounding Llyn Efyrnwy (Lake Vyrnwy). The N view, looking towards Bala, is largely of the sister peak Aran Benllyn. At 885m (2,905ft) this is the smaller of the two peaks and is part of the spiky ridge of cliffs 200m (656ft) high that extends beyond Creiglyn Dyfi. Aran Benllyn is a strongly recommended extension of this walk.

The way to Drysgol and the RAF memorial

Allow 1½ hours

From the summit of Aran Fawddwy you should retrace your steps SW to the L-stile and the fence that you followed earlier. After crossing the fence by the stile (MR 860220), change direction to head due S. This follows a further section of the fence on your L, heading for the large spur that is visible ahead. The ground is a stark contrast to the ascending route of Aran Fawddwy, being very

Indian summer on the summit of Aran Fawddwy.

rocky and steep. As you progress, the continuation of the steep E cliffs of Aran Fawddwy are approached. At the same time, although not visible as yet, the N side of Hengwm is also sweeping in towards the path such that it soon straddles the top of a narrow ridge. A few hundred paces from the summit of Aran Fawddwy the E cliffs are visible, and the complete lake of Creiglyn Dyfi can be seen for the first time. Beyond these are the cliffs that make up Aran Benllyn. The fence in front of you provides a useful barrier to the steep slopes that begin shortly after it. The path has now changed considerably and much of the rocky terrain has disappeared, to leave soft grass worn by sheep and walker. This terrain continues for most of the rest of the walk.

Ahead of you, looking SE, you should be able to see a distinctive cairn on the apex of the ridge, before it changes direction to culminate in Drysgol 1km (⅝ mile) away. This cairn marks the narrowest section of this short ridge, a place called Drws Bach. When you eventually reach it – after 200 paces beyond the viewpoint for the E cliffs of Aran Fawddwy described earlier – you will notice that the cairn is actually a memorial. At its base there is a small metal plaque explaining that it is dedicated to the memory of a Royal Air Force member SAC Michael John Aspain. He was killed in a storm at this point in 1960 while training in the area. There is also a small visitors' book hidden from the weather at the cairn and, at the time of the author's last visit, a bottle of water too – particularly useful, as the section of the walk from Aran Fawddwy to Drysgol is devoid of streams if you forget your liquid refreshment. However, this refuge cannot be relied upon.

From the RAF memorial, continue following the fence to your L, on a bearing of due E. The steep sides of the ridge at Drws Bach become less severe as you progress along it. Meanwhile, the W side of the enormous valley of Hengwm comes into view to the S, along with the river, the Afon yr Hengwm, that meanders gracefully SW along its floor. The path is still very clear and climbs steadily on to the broad dome of the curious peak of Drysgol, which is covered in lush grass. In addition to the vale of Hengwm, the main view of interest from here is

the exhilarating peep into the nameless cwm below the cliffs of Gwaun y Llwyni, looking WSW. This is a steep-sided corrie of which the upper slopes are mostly scree. You may also be able to see a precarious path traversing the S side of the cwm. This path leads around the NW side of the cwm to cross Pen Main, the view of which will develop as you progress down Hengwm.

The way along Hengwm and back to Cwm Cywarch
Allow 1 hour

As you walk over the rise of Drysgol, you will approach an L-stile and gate a few paces after crossing the eroded edge of a grassy plain. Take care when using this stile because it is not robust. Some 50 paces further on, the path diverges from the fence and changes from grass to shale. Due to the poor drainage of the descent from the S side of Drysgol the ground can become very wet, even after periods of drought. Eventually the path divides (MR 875205), with a smaller version continuing SE towards Waun Goch, while the more distinct path changes course suddenly to head SW. Follow the latter, which descends via the S side of Hengwm.

After the brief plateau of the NE end of Hengwm, as the path continues to descend, you will pass a waymarker and small guide in a framed, weatherproof stand which faces away from you. This view of the meandering river is now at its best, and it appears to be tied in knots in places. The path of the S side of Hengwm is very straight and clear, and using it as a descending route is a good choice because of the view of the valley that accompanies it. The descent is almost completely straight, except for folds in the hillside caused by three large tributaries to the Afon yr Hengwm. The path at these places is severely eroded, even though the water is guided by a short length of large-radius concrete piping in each case.

A few paces after the first of the tributaries you will need to cross a fence, which descends steeply right to the valley floor at Hafoty'r Hengwm (Hengwm summerhouse). There is an L-stile here which the sheep tend to shun in favour of burrowing underneath. To your R, looking due W, the full perspective of Pen Main is in view. Notice the unusual, regular trapezium shape of this rounded hill. While you study the views that open in front of you the path will become enveloped in short, dense ferns. Looking towards Hafoty'r Hengwm, at the head of the valley you will notice a small building and a flat area of the valley floor. On this plateau the points of the compass are depicted, drawn out in boulders; a quick glance at your compass will confirm that this curious feature is accurate as well as peculiar! The gentle descent continues, mostly on worn grass and dirt with the occasional tributary crossing the path, making the surrounding area quite muddy.

The straightness of the path is lost about 1km (⅝ mile) beyond the last L-stile encountered. This occurs when the path crosses a fence via another L-stile, into an open field that slopes gently away from the path and is usually host to cattle. The path is twice as wide as it was prior to the stile. After about 100 paces you will need to ford a shallow stream, beyond which is a small field full of tall thistles and a lone hawthorn tree. The field quickly narrows as you progress along the path, and a fence, preceded by a shallow ditch, joins the path to the R. A short distance further on there are many more deciduous trees – mainly mountain ash and hawthorn – to the R. After another 50 paces or so you will reach another L-stile, this time to the R of an aluminium gate and set in reeds and marshy ground.

Following the stile, the path becomes considerably narrower as it delves into the trees and leads to another metal gate within 100 paces. Just before the gate (which leads to a field and is not part of the path) the path strikes off to the R and descends much more rapidly to the SW. The soft grass of the path changes to hard, worn ground with a high rock content. This part of the route is quickly enveloped in trees, mostly the hawthorns that cover much of this section of Cwm Cywarch. The path descends quickly amid the tunnel of branches and you will pass a derelict farm building to the L. After about 200 paces, the path breaks out into the open and then turns sharply to the R. There is a P-stile to the L at this turning, which leads over a wooden fence in a SE direction towards Dinas Mawddwy and should be disregarded. After a few paces of comparatively flat walking almost due N, the path turns sharply to the L and again heads SW. The trees form another tunnel and the path follows between the high banks of their roots on either side. You will pass an array of cattle pens on the L, together with another derelict building. Immediately after these, some distance away in a meadow there is an antique rusty tractor near a hedgerow. Only a few paces further on along the path you will reach the river of the Afon Cywarch. There is a substantial footbridge to the R, or you can wade across the shallow, man-made concrete ford directly ahead. This leaves you on the path of ascent just a couple of hundred paces from the start of the walk and the car park.

Alternative routes

ESCAPES
This walk does not provide for any realistic short cuts, mainly because the summit ridge is long and too wet to cut across safely. The descent of Hengwm is the quickest return route, unless you decide to return by the route of ascent.

EXTENSIONS
There is a particularly worthwhile extension to this walk which, since it is already long, must be considered carefully! The extension begins at the summit of Aran Fawddwy and proceeds due N from the triangulation point, continuing along the ridge towards Aran Benllyn for 2km (1¼ miles). The ground is very rocky and loose but the path is still clear. You will lost height quickly and descend to a rather wet saddle between the mountains. From this point the height remains approximately constant, undulating gently along the ridge, which is sheer to the E. There is no triangulation point on the summit of Aran Benllyn (885m/2,905ft), but there is a summit cairn near a few small ponds. From this point you should retrace your steps due S to Aran Fawddwy and proceed via Drysgol, as described for the main route.

Route 15: THE BLACK MOUNTAIN

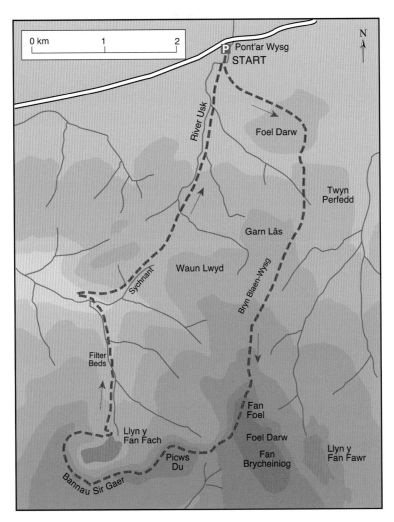

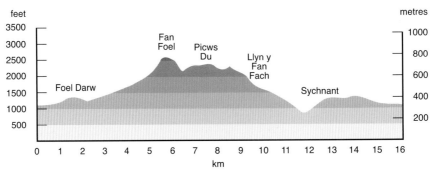

7

THE BRECON BEACONS

Route 15 • The Black Mountain

STARTING LOCATION
Car park at Pont'ar Wysg.
OLM 12/MR 820272.
Capacity for 25 cars with more parking available across the bridge on the R of the road.
No toilets.

ALTERNATIVE STARTING LOCATION
None.

PUBLIC TRANSPORT
None.

OVERVIEW/INTEREST
Complete traverse of the N ridge of the Black Mountain area.
Superlative scenery including expansive moorland and heath, sweeping grassy slopes and exposed cliff-tops.
Investigates prehistoric stone circle en route and passes the source of the River Usk.

Opportunity to observe wild ponies and several species of rare birds of prey including buzzards, kites and kestrels.
Returns via a pretty valley near Llanddeusant.

FOOTPATHS
Paths are not reliable for the complete walk, there is confusion with multiple sheep tracks and a compass is essential in all weathers.
Ridge walk is clear and easy but very exposed and dangerous in places.
Sections of the route follow clear service tracks.
Ascent of Fan Foel requires care due to mapping uncertainties.

GRADING   Difficult
TIME ALLOWANCE   7½ hours
DISTANCE Excluding height 17km (10.6 miles)
TOTAL HEIGHT GAINED   1,051m (3,447ft)
PRINCIPAL HEIGHTS
Fan Foel 781m (2,563ft)
Picws Du 749m (2,458ft)
Bannau Sir Gaer 677m (2,222ft)

The way to Fan Foel
Allow 3 hours

The Black Mountain area of the Brecon Beacons dominates the W section of the national park. In general, it is a huge, featureless expanse of high moorland. It is windswept and, in severe weather, offers few favours to the walker. However, it is also an incredibly beautiful area of the national park, more isolated than the popular haunts of Pen y Fan and just as spectacular. The main feature lies where the rolling planar expanse is interrupted by the impressive massif topped by Fan Foel, Fan Brycheiniog and Picws Du. This ridge, some 5km (3 miles) in length, is clearly visible from the N at a distance of 6km (3¾ miles) – almost from the car park where this walk begins.

The car park at Pont'ar Wysg is well hidden in the fir trees of the Glasfynydd Forest. This forest surrounds the banks of the Usk reservoir to the N and stretches over the small hill of Mynydd Wysg to the E. The small road that leaves from Trecastle is straight and flat and crosses the forest at a narrow section, about 1km (⅝ mile) across. The car park is on the L just as the forest gives way to the open heathland that extends to the N of the Black Mountain area. If you cross a cattle grid on your journey to the car park from Trecastle, you have gone too far!

From the car park, you need to walk back to the road and continue towards the cattle grid that is situated a few paces to the W. Use the K-gate to the L of the grid and turn immediately sharp L. The River Usk meanders in a wide ditch to the R which continues N, passing under a sophisticated road bridge to the rear. There is a narrow, clear path lying just to the R of the boundary fence of the forest, which runs along the banks of the river that now flows below and to the R of you. The path trundles along economically, sometimes on grass and sometimes along the tops of old, derelict drystone walling. The sodden ground encourages reeds and other marsh grasses on either side of the path.

After about 100 paces, the path deviates across a small plateau and leaves the shelter of the forest to seek out a route between two high banks ahead. It is a common feature of this area of the Brecon Beacons that the ground is shaped into the broad curves of small spurs, apparently pinned down by the small streams and rivers of the moor. The Usk presents a good example of this, with its huge banks carving a lengthy wandering channel N. The path becomes sandy as it continues S and pulls away from a gentle meandering tributary of the Usk to the R. A few hundred paces further on, the path meets the combination of fence and drystone wall that bounds the forest and undulates gradually uphill. It also turns gradually to the E, faithfully following the forest boundary. The boulders from the derelict drystone walls are strewn across a wide area and the ground is artificially rocky because of this. Otherwise, the terrain is predominantly of grass and damp marsh, and is easy on the feet.

You should now be glimpsing the first views of the small hill to the SE that is called Foel Darw (424m/1,392ft). This hill is fortunately placed, since it is significant in the surrounding flat land and is close enough to provide a useful navigational aid in poor visibility. You should continue to the L of this and head ESE. In places you will follow the banks of the Usk tributary again, but as you pass Foel Darw this will disappear and the open moorland surrounds you. The path crosses another derelict drystone wall and gradually leaves the forest on the L to a distance of about 500 paces. As you progress you will find that the path becomes more distinct; however, there are many sheep in the area and their tracks conspire to confuse, so keep the forest to your L, heading ESE. You will find there is also forest ahead of you and you will approach some modern sheepfolds. These are shown on the map at MR 830262.

Pass the R of the sheepfolds, heading towards the smooth, rolling, higher ground ahead to the S. You might find that there are many sheep who stand and appear curious as they did when the author prepared the route. Try not to disturb them, and if necessary trim your route slightly to avoid them. You will cross a ditch and then join a much better path worn by the four-wheeled bikes used by the shepherds in the area. This wide track proceeds at about 60 paces from the forest on your L, and you will soon come over the small rise that is the E flank of Foel Darw. From this position the view of the ground ahead is improved and you should be able to make out a slightly skew crossroads at MR 828256. The correct route is subtly waymarked with red and white arrows that are raggedly painted on boulders and rocks along this section of the way. However, you do not need to depend on these and they serve at best to provide reassurance as you continue. You should be heading SW as you descend towards the crossroads of paths, which is situated at the bottom of a pronounced dip in the moorland. This is formed by the combination of slopes from Foel Darw to the N and Twyn Perfedd to the SE. At the crossroads, head SSE along the path, which turns to head due S within a few paces. You will then pass a small river running a short distance to the R and after a few hundred paces will approach more sheepfolds, also on the R of the path. Make sure there is high ground to the L (Twyn Perfedd) and that you are progressing steadily uphill towards Garn Lâs.

Just after the second group of sheepfolds (MR 828253) you will cross the river, seen earlier on your R, in a small depression. The path continues to be wide and clear, but the ground is still very sodden for most of the year, even in severe droughts. You might be fortunate and see some of the wild ponies that live on the lower slopes of the N areas of the Black Mountain; they tend to whinny with a loud, shrill tone that can be heard over considerable distances. The red and white waymarkers continue for a short while and you will pass a large, flat cairn to your R, among the moorland and its scattered clumps of reeds.

Pay particular attention to the flattened cairn, since it is at this point (MR 829250) that the path heads off SSW for some distance. In clear weather, navigation is assisted by the spectacular view that is unfolding ahead. Much of the Black Mountain ridge is visible, resembling a vast monument amid the expanse of grass and moor. You are heading for the steep, flat-topped edge that is best identified by the sharp, narrow spur that sweeps down to the moorland, directly SSW of your present position. In mist you must rely on your compass, as the path loses much of its definition a short distance further on and, since there are many intricate sheep tracks present, simply following the current path is a challenge. You will be walking gradually uphill for more than 2km (1¼ miles) as you cross the slopes of Garn Lâs towards the steeper spur of Bryn Blaen-Wysg. The spongy clumps of grass that encroach on to the path will make walking more difficult: they tend to stretch your insteps, which can be uncomfortable. By continuing on the SSW bearing you will pass another flat cairn, to your L at the top of a slight rise.

Several hundred paces further on you will have gained considerable height, and expanses of moorland will fall away gently on both sides as you trudge up Bryn Blaen-Wysg. The path begins to improve (presumably due to walkers getting down to the serious business of the ascent of Fan Foel) before dividing at MR 824235. Since this is the start of a loop in the path, the choice of fork is not important. However, if you take the R fork you will pass through an ancient stone circle a few hundred metres further on.

The stone circle at MR 823232 is cunningly hidden among the lumpy grass and you should not expect Stonehenge! Locating it is also complicated by the few rocks scattered about, which can confuse. Even so, it is not difficult to locate, as the path is quite clear and passes directly through it, and you should look out for a semi-ordered set of stones a few metres across. As you will doubtless realize when you find the circle, it in fact consists of two concentric rings of low-lying boulders. Although interesting, the circle(s) is not a good navigational aid as its position on the map is dubious: it may be much closer to the slope of Tro'r Fan Foel (the Twist of Fan Foel) than indicated. Consequently, you should see the impressive slopes of Picws Du and Fan Foel shooting upwards from the flat moorland without warning. From the stone circle you should not head any further W, as this leads you along the lower reaches of these slopes. Instead, head SSE up the steep slope to your L.

Continue until you meet the definite path that heads due S up the edge called Gwely Ifan y Rhiw. In clear weather, the distinct appearance of Fan Foel should make this section easy (although a short, sharp climb is involved); however, in mist it can become dangerous. This is because on either side of the sharp spur there are fresh landslips and screes on very steep and difficult slopes. Hence, you should continue SE for as long as you gain height and then head due S for the summit. If you encounter any landslips or screes – their characteristic purple-red colour being due to the underlying sandstone – you have probably tracked too far W and need to trim your route accordingly. Thankfully, after much fumbling with a wet compass and flapping map, the author reached the summit without undue trouble in extremely poor visibility. The climb is quick and the summit of Fan Foel (781m/2,563ft) is reached within a couple of hundred paces.

The views from Fan Foel are impressive, yet offer only a brief preview in comparison with what is to follow. You will be able to look out across the moorland that you have crossed to the N and can see the Glasfynydd Forest beyond. To the S there is more heathland, and an undulating array of hills adopting grey and blue hues in the distance. Looking to the W there is the first view along the ridge itself: a series of sweeping, grassy spurs stretching almost to the horizon. These are explored next.

The way to Picws Du and Bannau Sir Gaer

Allow 2 hours

It is important not to stray further S than is required on Fan Foel, since the long plateaux beyond the summit turn into a wilderness in mist. Keep fairly close to the edge on your R and head SSW, taking care as there are precipitous crags just beyond the apparently harmless grassy slope to the R. This is a popular section of the route and the path is clear, with the exposed, windswept conditions making the terrain firm and clear. You will walk on the flat for a couple of hundred paces before the ridge starts to descend to the central saddle of the massif. The wide, grassy slope to the saddle of Nentydd Blaen-Trwch is called Bwlch Blaen-Trwch and provides a superlative view of the E side of Picws Du. This perspective comprises a huge green flank descending gradually to the S to join with the plateau of Carnau Gwys, while to the N the elements have torn away the surrounding land to leave steep crags uppermost, which lead to red sandstone screes further down. In summer there are usually several huge birds of prey soaring around the summit and the cliffs nearby; these are mainly buzzards that tend to quarrel in mid-air, but keep an eye out for the occasional lone kite that also frequents the area. The best views are to be had from Bwlch Blaen-Trwch before you lose too much height, and these include more distant sights of Carnau Llwydion to the W. This is a good place for a break to take in the impressive views all around.

The path descends to and crosses the deep, eroded gully, and with little respite starts to tackle

The last remnants of morning mist clear on Picws Du.

the E ascent of Picws Du. This follows a steep, grassy path that is once more quite close to the edge. Behind you, the opposing views of Bwlch Blaen-Trwch, the NW crags of Fan Foel and the continuing slopes of Cefn Bryn y Fuwch soon develop. To the S views of the impressive jumble of ridges and rises throughout the rolling landscape begin to fall away. The path does not become too steep and is also stepped in places, but it does venture very close to the exposed edge on the R so take care, especially with young walkers. When you are about 200 paces from the summit the cairn should come into view and the gradient relents for the last few steps to the top. The erosion is replaced here by hardy grass and sandstone.

The summit of Picws Du is wide and triangular in plan, protruding from the massif of the Black Mountain to the N. This enables the mountaineer to view not only the impressive sights to the E of Fan Foel and Fan Brycheiniog (significant because of the triangulation point), but also the new vistas to the W. The latter are arguably more impressive: looking

The view across Llyn y Fan Fach to Bannau Sir Gaer.

along the descending ridge, your eye is led to the sweeping cliffs of Bannau Sir Gaer and the lake of Llyn y Fan Fach, which hides in the shelter that the cliffs provide, and all the abrupt and jagged crags are neatly blended with the plateaux that make up the lower slopes. You may see buzzards dogfighting around the tidy, ordered cliffs of Cwar-du-mawr, unperturbed by the mountain's flightless visitors.

From the summit, continue SW, in fine weather this should be simple, since you just follow the ridge. In mist, as before, care is required because of the hazardous cliffs. After proceeding SW along the gently descending grassland for 0.5km (⅓ mile), the path (together with the ridge) turns due W and continues for the next 1km (⅝ mile). This section is particularly exhilarating, as the view of Bannau Sir Gaer is outstanding and accompanies you for much of the high-level walking. There is also the lake of Llyn y Fan Fach far below to the R. As you pass this feature the path will skirt around a gully of loose shale and begin to follow the ridge around to the N. You will find that the path actually skirts the top of Bannau Sir Gaer; it is your choice as to whether you deviate slightly to the W to cross the summit (MR 797215). This is easy, as it is only a short distance away, However, arguably the best views await as you begin to head due N following Bannau Sir Gaer. This is because the complete N ridge of the Black Mountain stretches out in front of you from this position (MR 796217). One of the most comprehensive and picturesque views in Wales, it comprises the inky-blue waters of Llyn y Fan Fach in the foreground, the slopes of Pwll yr Henllyn and the cliffs below Picws Du in the middle ground, and a background dominated by the long, steep spur of Fan Foel. To the N, there is the now familiar expanse of moorland. Beyond this, looking NNE, you might be able to make out the forest where the walk began. Have a rest here before you head back!

The way back to Pont'ar Wysg

Allow 2½ hours

From the viewpoint just N of Bannau Sir Gaer, proceed N until the path divides. Here you should disregard the L fork that heads NE and continue along the path to the R, which heads due E. This path quickly descends the few hundred metres to the N side of the lake, possibly still accompanied by the distant call of a buzzard from the summit of Picws Du. At the lakeside there is a small pump-house, a dam and a narrow weir. There are shimmering sights across the lake towards the cliffs of Bannau Sir Gaer and Cwar-du Bach; in the afternoon these lie in shade and appear black and austere. From the pump-house, proceed due N along the rubble track that is used to service the dam. Disregard the similar track leaving to the E, as this just connects two other weirs further along.

From Llyn y Fan Fach, the rubble track takes you to a pretty Welsh vale that is quiet and undisturbed. This valley has been formed by the river leaving the dam but has no name. The slope on the left is called Llethr y Llyn, which develops

into Waun y Llyn as you proceed along the track. The river (which will eventually become the Afon Sawdde) is very clean and bubbles in and out of the occasional man-made weir and enclosure, over rich green algae and moss. You will pass some rusty railings to the R and the cliffs quickly recede behind you. After 1km (⅝ mile) you will pass a sloosh pool and some filter beds, shown on the map at MR 803230. There is a locked gate across the rubble track ahead and the footpath continues on the R, up the bank beyond the drystone wall. This short diversion is waymarked as 'Llymbr' (footpath) but when the author last visited the sign was broken. After only a few paces you will rejoin the loose rubble service track once more, past a similar waymarker to that encountered earlier.

Ahead of you is a small hill which is unnamed. The route eventually traverses along the bottom of this spur as it begins to cross the moorland again. However, at present it continues to follow the R bank of the river for several hundred paces. After this the track meanders slightly to the W and crosses several bridges, as a small wood comes into view to the W. This wood signifies the beginning of the valley of Llanddeusant. The road crosses a more significant bridge that has black-and-white bollards, and immediately turns L. On your R you will see the steep, grassy slope of the small hill seen earlier; within a couple of hundred paces you should notice a path heading due E along a contour of this hill. It is quite clear and leaves before the woodland begins. This path forms a hairpin with the road and you should follow it as it climbs, gradually, on a diagonal traverse out of Llanddeusant.

Your legs might be slightly reluctant to climb at this stage of the walk and will protest in the usual manner! The climb is not steep, but it is reasonably long and passes through a great deal of gorse on either side. Several sheep tracks and paths that are not shown on the map will eventually join from the L and the path continues on its rocky and sandy way, turning gradually to head NE after a few hundred paces. It proceeds in parallel to the river of Sychnant below to the R. Within a few hundred paces your route is crossed by a couple of paths, the latter of which is shown on the map (MR 809243). This is located adjacent to the source of

Sychnant, which is identifiable by the end of the narrow valley it has formed through time. You will now almost have reached the large saddle between the unnamed hill to the W (460m/1,509ft) and Waun Lwyd to the E. Disregard both of these paths and continue NE as before along the faint path. The terrain is now similar to the beginning of the walk and the paths are not to be trusted, so follow your compass. You might notice another stone circle as you proceed: again small, overgrown boulders almost denying any regular structure until you study them carefully.

After this the moorland falls away gently in front of you and you are looking down the shallow valley formed by the early stages of the River Usk (its source is to the E of Waun Lwyd, as indicated on the map). Before you make your way down the slopes to the Usk, remember to look behind you at the complete massif of the Black Mountain, as much of it quickly becomes obscured by the intermediate moorland. The range appears very distant and the effect of the afternoon sunlight makes the cliffs and upper slopes appear black and haunting. The ridge is long and a challenge for many camera lenses, rising in the E to Fan Brycheiniog and Fan Foel to fall steadily to the lower peaks of Picws Du and Bannau Sir Gaer.

A bearing of NE will guide you across stubbly grass, moorland and some marsh. There are paths here and there left by the sheep and these serve well to avoid much of the sodden ground. Within 1km (⅝ mile) you will reach the River Usk in its deep, narrow gorge. You need to cross this narrow watercourse at one of the several accessible places along its banks. Around the Usk you may encounter quite large groups of wild ponies, who use the river for watering.

Continue along the E bank of the Usk and follow it for the remaining steps of the return route. It proceeds on a bearing of NNE and there is a much more reliable path along its banks here than was available earlier. From the first stages of this descent via the river's meandering loops and bends, there is an enigmatic view of Fan Brycheiniog to the S. Somewhat fortuitously, this escarpment is located so that it stands behind you over the Usk as you follow it N.

You will find that the path weaves in and out of the grassland and scattered clumps of reeds as it follows the river. It climbs high on the banks of the river and you will need to cross several muddy gullies where tributaries join the Usk, for example at the in-flow of the Nant Llyswennod. After almost 2km (1¼ miles) the path descends positively down a short, steep slope to approach the river to the L and you will find you are between the steep banks where the path forked L to follow the forest, close to the start of the walk. You should now retrace your steps back to the car park in the shade of the tall conifers.

There is a picnic table in the woods, visible from the car park, which is an ideal place to stop for refreshments and conclude your adventurous walk in the Black Mountain.

Alternative routes

ESCAPES

If the weather deteriorates severely, the safest escape prior to Picws Du is to return by the outgoing route. The scenery and potentially treacherous moorland require good visibility, so this will be a sensible short cut if the skies do not clear. Otherwise, there are no short cuts beyond Picws Du and you must persevere along the recommended route.

EXTENSIONS

A small extension to this walk is to include the peak of Fan Brycheiniog (802m/2,631ft). To do this, continue SSE along the E cliffs from Fan Foel, taking great care in mist as the cliffs are interrupted by deep gullies 100m (328ft) deep. Within a few hundred paces you will be able to see the triangulation point that indicates the summit, about 500m (542yd) from Fan Foel.

From Fan Brycheiniog you can either return to Fan Foel and continue as recommended in the main route, or traverse due W down to the saddle of Bwlch Blaen-Trwch and continue from there. The latter option omits some of the impressive views described earlier but is the most direct continuation route.

119

Route 16: PEN Y FAN, CORN DU AND CRIBYN FROM THE NORTH

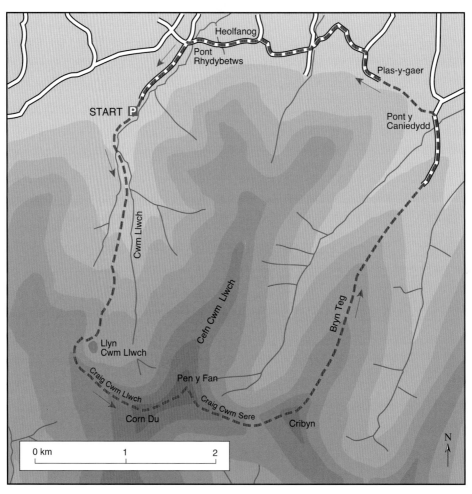

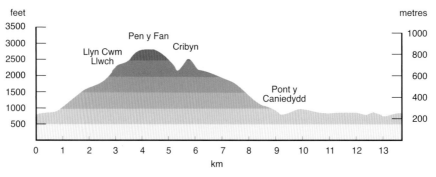

Route 16 • Pen y Fan, Corn Du and Cribyn from the North

STARTING LOCATION
Large car park at Cwm Llwch (prone to crime so secure vehicles well).
OLM 11/MR 006244.
No toilets.

ALTERNATIVE STARTING LOCATION
None.

PUBLIC TRANSPORT
None.

OVERVIEW/INTEREST
Spectacular ascent of three major peaks in the Brecon Beacons.
Vast combinations of valley and ridge.
Breathtaking scenery and panoramic views of the surrounding regions.
Visits the isolated lake of Llyn Cwm Llwch and the Tommy Jones memorial obelisk.
Pleasant return route through peaceful lowlands.

FOOTPATHS
Route is clear throughout, with limited waymarking.
Paths are eroded sand and loose rock.
Grassy ridges and summits are exposed and dangerous with steep slopes.
Descent of Cribyn is steep, loose and exposed, requiring care and concentration.

GRADING Difficult
TIME ALLOWANCE 6½ hours
DISTANCE
Excluding height 14.5km (9.1 miles)
TOTAL HEIGHT GAINED 1,049m (3,440ft)
PRINCIPAL HEIGHTS
Corn Du 873m (2,865ft)
Pen y Fan 886m (2,908ft)
Cribyn 795m (2,609ft)

The way to Llyn Cwm Llwch   *Allow 1 hour*

The car park at Cwm Llwch is situated in the remarkably flat N area of the cwm, with the Afon Llwch to the E – a river almost completely hidden by the trees that shroud its banks. The car park is next to a campsite, and in all but the harshest of weathers you will probably see a few tents pitched in the shadow of the Brecon Beacons, visible through the surrounding trees to the S. The land to the E, beyond the river, is used for cattle. To the W, the large, flat meadows accommodate wild ponies. The atmosphere in this car park is both tranquil and refreshing, and it makes a perfect starting point.

Start the walk by proceeding SW along the wide gravel track that passes through the car park. You will see various signs and notices indicating 'No motors' and 'Fire risk', and will pass a large meadow on your L where ponies usually graze, normally in family groups of two adults and their young. The path is made up of sand and bedrock, and at this stage is flat. There is an impressive variety of trees on both sides of the track including ash, hawthorn, beech, sycamore and hazel. After a few hundred metres you will pass a signpost for Cwm Llwch in the direction you are heading, and the gradient gradually increases. Through the trees on the L the small spur of Twn y Dyfnant can be seen, possibly in silhouette due to the morning sunshine in the E. You will pass another waymarker on the R, and after a further few hundred metres the path crosses a stream via a wooden footbridge with twin railings. You will then need to use a P-stile to the L of a metal gate while the yellow-arrowed waymarkers continue. A few paces further on the trees to the L separate slightly and Pen y Fan can be viewed through the clearing to the S.

The Brecon Beacons are majestic mountains. To the experienced North Wales' mountaineer they offer more expansive scenery of sweeping lines, but with all the exhilaration found elsewhere. The Beacons themselves are the highest points of a massive plateau that stretches to the s over several kilometres. The N extent of this landscape is made up of an orderly array of wide valleys and extensive spurs that reach out towards the town of Brecon. The tops of these spurs join the plateau at peaks that have been spared the erosion of the lower slopes. The four main peaks – Corn Du, Pen y Fan, Cribyn and the more E Fan y Big – are indeed beacons along the ridge, and they hold a symmetry that will become more apparent as the walker explores further.

The path continues by following a groove between drystone walls, while on the right is another meadow occupied by thistles and more docile ponies. The recommended path follows to the R around a farmyard and a long white cottage (MR 005238). The path joins the main track again after a P-stile and you now enter open country, the views of Corn Du and Pen y Fan becoming even more spectacular to the s. The path steepens considerably and climbs a wide, grassy slope while weaving between scattered deciduous trees and narrowing slightly. As you progress the path develops and straightens, occupying an eroded, rutted gully between trees with ferns on the lower banks. The views improve further, with most of Cwm Llwch now visible. Directly ahead you should be able to see a rather square cairn several hundred paces away. Beyond this, the rise of the ground obscures the lake hidden beyond the pronounced ridge and the associated N slopes of Craig Cwm Llwch. This edge rises gradually to the E, up to the angular summit of Corn Du (873m/2,865ft). The ridge continues to rise to the higher summit of Pen y Fan (886m/2,908ft), while to the w of Craig Cwm Llwch there is a lesser peak which is unnamed. On the R of the path, looking

In the woodlands of Cwm Llwch, looking towards Corn Du.

due W, you might be able to pick out the disused targets that were originally used for army training. Meanwhile, the trees will become sparser as you gain more height.

A few hundred paces further on, you will approach a fence that is crossed by a P-stile with a rusty gate to the R. Immediately after this, there is a National Trust sign denoting the beginning of the Cwm Llwch area. There is a considerable amount of scattered slate debris just above you, shed from the large cairn that marks the head of the rise. As your preceding steps have been over steep ground, and there is a pleasant view N of the valley towards Brecon, this spot presents a good place for a breather. As you progress, either rested or breathing hard, the ground will flatten out just beyond the cairn and the path becomes more worn with dirt and sand exposed through the flattened grass. The flat area is waymarked by the occasional cairn, which is particularly helpful in poor weather conditions.

The flat area leads closer to the N slopes of Craig Cwm Llwch that have suffered landslips in the past. These have torn away strips of vegetation, revealing the vermilion sandstone beneath; this is a common characteristic of the Brecon Beacons. Above the slopes, on top of the ridge, there is a small obelisk that will be investigated shortly. When the path forks by a large and flat cairn (MR 003224) after a few hundred paces, you should take the L fork which heads for the lake. This disregards the path that strikes off up on to the rim of the cwm. You will pass several rocks and boulders protruding through the grassy terrain and will approach the area in which the river from the lake (as yet not visible) leaves via a deep groove in the surrounding dish. Deep fissures in the N slopes of Corn Du and Pen y Fan can be seen from this position. Following a brutish climb over the rim of the corrie, there is a short, gentle descent to the lakeside and another well-earned rest!

Llyn Cwm Llwch is a small, sheltered lake that is surrounded by the steep slopes of Craig Cwm Llwch. There is a path around the perimeter which is well worth exploring, as there are interesting views from the far shores of the lake. The surrounding grassy hillocks to the S make this a peaceful location and a valuable oasis in summer.

The way to Corn Du and Pen y Fan

Allow 2½ hours

The path continues to the W and because of its eroded nature is visible following a zigzag route up the steep slopes above the lake. The path begins as a grassy, comfortable track but quickly surrenders this in favour of the red sand beneath as the gradient increases. The route becomes very steep and has been stepped in places to assist the walker, presumably by the National Trust. The first bend of the staggered ascent is decorated by a large pile of rocks, maybe for use in future erosion treatment, and in dry weather the sand can be quite loose underfoot. The steps are shallow but height is gained quickly nonetheless, and the lake rapidly recedes to a small, distant pool far below. This aerobic torture is eased for a few paces until a section of larger steps is reached and the gradient soars again! This lasts for a short while until the top of the ridge is gained, where another path joins from the R – this is the path from the R fork disregarded earlier in favour of the route via the lake.

The combined path is clear and well worn, bending around to head SE while passing a small obelisk hewn from a hunk of granite. This monument tells a desperate, haunting tale from the turn of the century. The stone is dedicated to a toddler, Tommy Jones, who at five years of age lost his way while walking the short distance from Cwm Llwch to Login in 1900. After 29 days his body was found at the site of the obelisk, which was erected in memorial the following year.

From the obelisk, the path continues SE along Craig Cwm Llwch towards the distant heights of Corn Du (SE) and Pen y Fan (E). To begin with the climb is gradual and comfortable, and the path narrows while becoming more exposed on the L. As encountered earlier on this route, the severe erosion has caused the path to sink into a narrow groove. To the SW smooth, grassy slopes come into view for the first time and are in striking contrast with the steep, plunging cwms of the N. Beyond the grassy slopes several peaks are visible from your present position dominated by Fan Fawr (734m/2,408ft).

An additional path joins the ridge path from the w and you will pass a National Trust sign indicating areas of revegetation and instructing you to 'Keep to the path'. At this stage the gradient increases considerably, and minor watercourses traverse the path via man-made channelling. The steepness of the path has caused its route to fragment slightly and it is therefore wide and sandy, once more verified by the occasional cairn. As it becomes ever steeper (your lungs will bear witness!), the path meanders gently to reduce the effort required. This does not appear to work very well, since the climb subsequently develops into an absolute onslaught, the worst section indicated by the 200m (217yd) of National Trust path that completes the ascent. The path remains very exposed and close to the edge of Craig Cwm Llwch, until it turns a short distance to the R and then L to clamber on to the flat summit of Corn Du up a narrow, rocky approach. From this position you can observe other bewildered walkers

The memorial to Tommy Jones who perished here in 1900.

struggling for breath amid sighs of relief as they reach the summit: the climb is considerably more daunting than indicated by the map.

The flat, triangular summit of Corn Du has a craggy sheer face to the N, while to the s it slopes away gently to the saddle of Bwlch Duwynt and the ridges of Craig Gwaun Taf and Cefn Crew beyond. Much of the view is obscured by the extent of the summit and you will need to wander around to fully appreciate the surrounding countryside. To the w the summit of Pen y Fan lies only a few hundred paces away along the ridge, while in the distance behind it are Cribyn and Fan y Big, the subsequent summits as you head E. On the E horizon lies the long, flat mountain of Waun Rydd, and in summer sunshine the distant shimmer fromthe Upper Neuadd reservoir can be seen to the

SE. The summit Corn Du is a popular sun-trap in the summer, but in the depths of winter is transformed into a bleak and hostile outpost.

When you have absorbed the magnificent views, you should leave the summit of Corn Du heading due E. There is a variety of paths heading in this direction and they all undertake a gradual turn towards the N as they develop. You will cross a few rock slabs and the view of the reservoir improves to the SE. In mist, take extreme care and remain vigilant of the steep, precipitous slopes to the N, but do not lose more height than is absolutely necessary as you should quickly reach the saddle between the two mountains. The path is very wide for a summit ridge and other routes will join it here and there. After about 200 paces the gradient increases suddenly and it is an easy climb to the summit of Pen y Fan. The summit has a wide, flat cairn and is of a similar size to that of Corn Du. The views are changed slightly, with the forest in the N depths of Cwm Sere to the NE and the long, narrow spur that heads N from the summit, Cefn Cwm Llwch, also visible. There is a long, sandy path along the top which can be seen for a considerable distance. The triangulation point was removed a few years ago.

The way to Cribyn and back to Cwm Llwch
Allow 3 hours

You should disregard the path that heads N along Cefn Cwm Llwch and instead head SE towards Cribyn, along Craig Cwm Sere. The distance between Pen y Fan and Cribyn is further than that between Corn Du and Pen y Fan and requires the loss of a great deal of height. Consequently, the descent from Pen y Fan, which follows the rocky edge of the ridge closely, is steeper and more severe with loose rock underfoot. There are signs warning of revegetation along the path, which winds steeply and is stepped in places. As on the ascent of Corn Du, there are several artificially channelled watercourses crossing the path, and because of the gradient you may find your legs running away with you towards Cribyn – a stark contrast with the ascent of Corn Du! The staggered N–S

arrangement of Corn Du and Pen y Fan makes it possible to view them both as you descend. The lower summit of Cribyn appears very small from your present position (MR 015214), but in reality this is not the case. It is observed as a wide, triangular ridge with the path a clear sandy scar across it. About 200 paces from the summit of Pen y Fan the path divides and you should keep L, sticking to the edge of the descending ridge. The R fork bypasses Cribyn to the S leading to Fan y Big, which is not included in this route. However, the most prominent ascent of Cribyn is about 100 paces from the edge, so you should alter your route slightly as you approach the saddle to meet up with this. The loose shale and red colour of the path means that this should cause few problems, even in poor visibility.

You will pass a flattened cairn on the R, before reaching the saddle between the mountains. This area can be marshy and wet, and the grass is thicker and more stubbly. To the L of Cribyn there is another path which traverses its N face, heading WNW. However, the recommended route continues up the W side of Cribyn due E and is unexpectedly steep and eroded. The path is restored in places and the author noticed a discarded wheelbarrow to the R of it on his last visit! The climb is demanding, especially at this stage of the walk, but is relatively short and the summit is achieved quickly. Be sure to take in the views behind you as you climb from the saddle, as the NE face of Pen y Fan is breathtaking, particularly in late afternoon sunshine. It comprises a colossal finely layered mass of sandstone covered in grass that is torn regularly in strips to reveal the red rock beneath. Where this has not occurred, the grass appears to shroud the rock like green velvet. The immense expanse of this geological feature is truly awe-inspiring.

The summit of Cribyn is much smaller than the preceding peaks and has a small, neat cairn. From the summit you can see the peaks explored earlier in the walk, as well as the great spur of Cefn Cwm Llwch that heads N from Pen y Fan. To descend, you must head NE. At first this may seem unreasonable, since the very first steps are down an extremely steep arête. It is naturally stepped and there tend to be loose, slippery fragments of sandstone throughout the eroded path, so care is required. You might need to use your hands occasionally and try to move one limb at a time to reduce the risk of slipping. This steep section lasts for about 200m (215yd), after which the grass reclaims much of the path and the walking is more relaxing and safer. Coincident with the reduction in gradient, a path joins from the L which is the traverse route of the N side of Cribyn, mentioned above. You can now enjoy the leisurely walk along the spur of Bryn Teg that is accompanied by the spurs of Cefn Cyff to the E and Cefn Cwm Llwch to the W. Looking N you can see Brecon and its surrounding farmland, while the peak of Fan y Big occupies the sheer slopes to the SE.

Bryn Teg is flat, grassy and wide. There are occasional cairns on the L which assist in bad weather, as the path is predominantly flattened grass at this stage. There are scattered tussocks of gorse among the grasses and after about 1km (⅝ mile) the path follows a wide divide between two areas of ferns. The land develops into a field with a few scattered boulders between drystone walls. These two walls gradually encroach upon the path, eventually meeting at a wooden gate directly ahead. Just before the gate there is a National Trust sign indicating the boundary of Cwm Cynwyn, the large valley east of Bryn Teg. After the gate the path is very different: it supports little vegetation and is made up of rubble, possibly forming a minor watercourse after heavy rainfall. In contrast to the open, windswept descent via Bryn Teg, the path is sheltered within an avenue of deciduous trees. These are mainly silver birch, rowan and ash. As you continue down the easy gradient you will pass a variety of metal and wooden gates to either side of the main track, and there are also some waymarkers. The paths served by all these should be ignored in favour of the major track, which becomes tarmac after a short distance. The trees eventually give way to hawthorn on the L and ferns on the verge of the R. You will pass another couple of metal gates on the L.

From a geographical point of view, the spur of Bryn Teg continues NE and the tarmac track follows it faithfully for a few hundred paces. Then, as the spur flattens and widens to meet the flat farmlands surrounding Brecon, the track falls to the L, heading due N. It descends into a deep cutting as it approaches the Nant Sere (the stream from Cwm Sere). This is crossed by means of the small, stone road bridge of Pont y Caniedydd (Bridge of the Singer). Following this there is a short, sharp incline and you should then turn L to reach a metal gate and P-stile immediately (MR 039245).

The rubble-strewn path served by the P-stile and gate is well used by farm vehicles and heads due W. It sweeps towards some isolated farm buildings ahead, which are derelict and overgrown, and then around to the L and over a small rise leading to Cwm Sere. On the L is an open meadow of grass the thistles, while the R of the path is banked with sapling trees. You should continue for only a couple of hundred paces, looking out for a waymarked path leaving the track to the R over a P-stile, just after a metal gate. Take care when using the stile as there is some exposed barbed wire. This path heads NW across a small field and is not very clear. However, if you keep the farm buildings to your L and cross the field diagonally, it is not too complicated. The connecting P-stile quickly comes into view at the top of the field, from where the next P-stile can be seen at the top L corner of the next field. The path develops gradually and becomes clearer, and a few paces further on you will cross another P-stile.

From the open meadows around Pont y Caniedydd, you again enter an area of deciduous trees along a neat path that skirts the top of an inclined meadow. The trees along this section provide shelter from the afternoon sunshine and throw their long shadows on to the meadow. It is best to keep to the perimeter of the small field, in the trees, until some more farm buildings can be seen to the NW. This is the small settlement of Plas-y-gaer. You need to head for these down a slight gradient, towards the rusty corrugated iron of an animal enclosure. When you approach the buildings you will find a P-stile and some bridlepath waymarkers that direct you through the farmyard. You will pass a converted rail wagon on your L and, following the waymarkers, turn immediately R; there are farm sheds ahead of you. Continue through the yard, through a metal gate (waymarked with a blue arrow) and follow the route on to a straight tarmac track, disregarding any preceding tracks and paths leaving to the L or R. You should then head NW for the next 200–300 paces or so.

The tarmac road leaving Pas-y-gaer to the NW is smooth and straight and crosses open country along a contour. After a few hundred paces you will pass a track heading SW towards the hill of Allt Ddu, which should be disregarded. This hill can be viewed to the SW through the few surrounding trees. As you pass this turning, the main track will turn gradually to head due N. About 200 paces further on the track you will meet another, more established tarmac road which is at a T-junction. Here (MR 032252) you should turn L.

The remainder of the route follows a quiet minor road for about 2km (1¼ miles), skirting the N end of Cefn Cwm Llwch – the last time the author walked the route, in a particularly busy summer, he was passed by only one vehicle! The narrow tarmac road is densely hedged in places and passes through an idyllic section where it is sheltered in a tunnel of trees. The road undulates gently over the remains of the long ridges from the Brecon Beacons; where the trees allow, these ridges, and Cefn Cwm Llwch in particular, can be viewed to the S. You will meet three junctions in all, at which you should always bear L. The first passes over a small stone bridge over a stream, close to farm buildings. This provides a good place for a rest, since you can sit on the wall of the bridge. The second junction is opposite the settlement of Heolfanog. Following this, the road descends once again into its pretty shroud of deciduous trees, to cross the river of Nant Cwm Llwch via the wide bridge of Pont Rhydybetws. This river is quite noisy because of the waterfall nearby and is itself covered by the branches of numerous trees. The third junction follows soon after a flat meadow on the L. Turn L here and then follow the track of rubble, which continues for about 1km (⅝ mile) back to the car park. On a hot summer's day the author can verify that the river which follows the edge of the car park provides the best refreshment for tired feet and salty brow!

Alternative routes

ESCAPES

The most obvious short cut is to descend from Pen y Fan due N, following the ridge of Cefn Cwm Llwch. This might be particularly useful if the weather deteriorates significantly and you do not wish to continue down the steep descent from Cribyn. After about 4km (2½ miles) on this path you will join the rubble track that was mentioned in the main route as being waymarked for Allt Ddu (MR 031247). This track joins the previous route just before the first junction of the tarmac road, and you can then follow the recommended route back to the car park.

EXTENSIONS

You may wish to include the fourth Beacon, Fan y Big, in your route. For this you need to descend due S from the summit of Cribyn, as opposed to NE as previously recommended. This extended route turns to head due W as it follows the edge of Craig Cwm Cynwyn towards the saddle of Bwlch ar y Fan at 599m (1,967ft). From this point there are impressive views of the forest-filled Cwm Cynwyn to the NNE and of the E side of Bryn Teg. To the S there are now much improved views of the Upper Neuadd reservoir and the extensive Taf Fechan forest beyond.

The descent from Cribyn via Craig Cwm Cynwyn is more gradual than that of Craig Cwm Sere (the descent from Pen y Fan described earlier). However, after this brief respite there is a short, steep climb to the long, broad summit of Fan y Big. From this position (MR 036206) you should head back to the saddle of Bwlch ar y Fan – you could follow the path along the top of Cefn Cyff, but this greatly extends the distance to be walked along minor roads. From the saddle, head N for not more than 100 paces. At this point (MR 032206) you should follow the path as it heads NW. This path follows the 500m (1,641ft) contour along the E side of Bryn Teg, eventually joining the original route at the wooden gate in Cwm Cynwyn (MR 036235). The straightness of the tarmac track is distinctive. You should then follow the recommended route back to the car park.

Route 17: GARN FAWR AND STRUMBLE HEAD

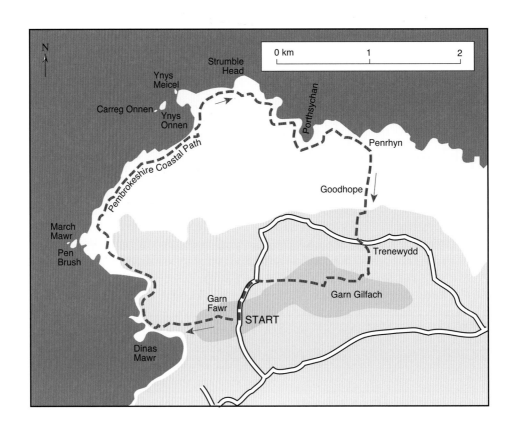

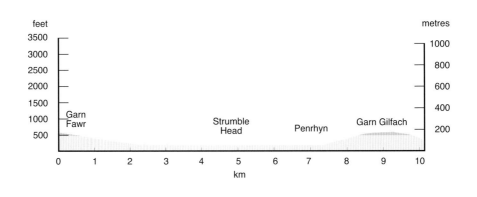

8

THE PEMBROKESHIRE COAST

Route 17 • Garn Fawr and Strumble Head

STARTING LOCATION
Car park at Garn Fawr.
OLM 35/MR 899388.
Capacity for 25 cars .
No toilets.

ALTERNATIVE STARTING LOCATION
None.

PUBLIC TRANSPORT
None.

OVERVIEW/INTEREST
Fantastic coastline scenery, idyllic secluded bays
    and precipitous cliff-tops.
Seals in isolated areas and plenty of birdlife.
Sunsets from Garn Fawr.
Passes the Strumble Head lighthouse.

FOOTPATHS
Paths are clear throughout, with periodic
    waymarking.
Coastal path is worn and dangerous in places, so
    keep hold of children.
Undulating coastline can be deceptive in distance
    covered.

GRADING Moderate
TIME ALLOWANCE 4 hours
DISTANCE
Excluding height 10.5km (6.6 miles)
TOTAL HEIGHT GAINED 213m (699ft)
PRINCIPAL HEIGHTS
Garn Fawr 213m (699ft)

The way to Garn Fawr and the Coastal Path
Allow ½ hour

This walk starts from the small car park situated on a slope between the outcrops of Garn Fawr (w) and Garn Fechan (beyond the road to the E). These small peaks are both sites of ancient forts and can be viewed from the start of the walk. The car park is surrounded by an overgrown drystone wall which gives way to the dense ferns and gorse that cover the lower slopes of both outcrops. The view beyond the rocky peaks is dominated by the expanse of patchwork farmland that extends to the horizon in the s.

Leave by the small path at the top (N) of the car park, which heads due w up a steady incline, away from the road. The ferns are very tall and the path follows a channel between them; there are also brambles and gorse. This dense thicket lasts for only a few hundred paces, however, and the path soon meets open country and becomes smooth and grassy. To the L large clumps of rock begin to obscure the view. A path will leave to the L, which you should disregard in favour of the steeper route to the w. There are occasional yellow-arrowed waymarkers along the path at this stage to assist you.

Just a few hundred paces from the car park the sea comes into view to the N, in summer sunshine it will appear a deep cyan, extending to the horizon. The path is wide and smooth, with borders of ferns guiding its way between crags and boulders. The view N gradually develops and you will soon be able to discern the lighthouse at

Strumble Head, distinctive due to its periodic flash of light across the land. Soon after this feature comes into view you will approach a triangulation point ahead. This marks the summit of Garn Fawr which, at a mere 213m (699ft), is a small but distinctive peak; it is clearly visible from much of the neighbouring coast path and from St David's and other settlements nearby. The summit is reached a short distance along the path, which follows a flat course for about 50m (54yd). It proceeds to the R, through a gap in a derelict drystone wall, to a short scramble up to the summit.

The views from Garn Fawr are superlative and it is strongly recommended that you choose good weather for this walk. To the SW there is a truly breathtaking scene of rugged Welsh coastline extending almost to St David's Head, some 20km (13 miles) away. This coastline weaves gracefully in and out of the smooth farmland, and the rich combination of pastel shades and deep marine blues and greens is captivating. The sea along this stretch is usually a little unruly and traces of white

A view of the coastline on the descent from Garn Fawr.

foam adorn the beaches. To the N, the view is different, in that it is in sharper perspective and culminates in the Strumble Head lighthouse. Looking E, there are more peaceful fields rolling down towards the harbour at Fishguard.

On the summit of Garn Fawr there is an inscription left by naval servicemen who occupied the now derelict and unrecognizable look-out post during past hostilities. This feature is not clear (indeed, the author missed it on his first visit) and it can elude you if you are in a hurry to continue the route. The sculpted words indicate the names and dates of those who looked out across this coastline many years ago.

From the summit you should continue due W; there is a tangle of paths for a few metres, after which a more defined path takes over and descends rapidly towards the coast. Remember to take your eyes off the beautiful coastal scenery occasionally, otherwise you may end up in the dense ferns (as did the author). The path surrenders height quickly and you will soon notice the aspect of Garn Fawr forming behind you, to the E. After a couple of hundred paces the path flattens as it approaches a P-stile, which is followed

by a small collection of buildings in and around Tal-y-Gaer Farm (MR 893388). The path crosses a tarmac road a short distance afterwards, heading towards the local youth hostel. Across the road the route turns almost immediately R, as indicated by signs for the Coastal Path. There are a couple of P-stiles to be climbed as the path winds its way gradually downhill through more ferns and brambles, towards a distinctive peninsula ahead. This feature is called Dinas Mawr and is another site of an ancient fort; there are an abundance of partially submerged rocks and the path flattens as it meets the coastline.

The way to Strumble Head and Porthsychan *Allow 2 hours*

The emerald waters of the Irish Sea accompany the next stage of the route and you should keep to the clearly defined Coastal Path wherever possible. There are numerous occasions where paths leave to the L to investigate peninsulas and stacks; Dinas Mawr is a typical example. You should take care if you follow these and always return to the Coastal Path before continuing N. The path is well-maintained and economic and there are few opportunities for short cuts.

After a brief inland section following the mêlée of Dinas Mawr, the path circumvents a delightful small bay named Porth Maenmelyn. The path descends appreciably and passes a P-stile, which should be disregarded, before climbing to the upper reaches of the opposite side of the bay. Beyond this the path crosses another section of inland higher ground to the L of some derelict red-brick buildings. These structures are steeped in thick gorse and heather and their purpose is not obvious; they are possibly more look-out posts like the remains of those on Garn Fawr, or maybe defunct mining buildings.

The path heads NW as it trails the coastline. Those brave enough to have worn shorts will certainly be cursing now, since the gorse is ruthless with tender ankles! The path climbs steadily past a few cairns, to the top of the high ground at 89m (292ft), which lies among a few outcrops. From this position (MR 883397) you can look out to sea

to the W, across the semi-islands of Pen Brush and March Mawr. The curse of the gorse continues and the path makes its way across occasional rock slabs, now zigzagging between N and NW. It also loses some definition but is regularly waymarked, even if the signs are getting a bit old and ragged.

The surrounding vegetation is generally gorse and ground-lying heather. These shrubs tend to flower at several times of the year, so the route is usually blessed with a variety of colour. However, it is worth taking your time as there are rarer flowers in among the crevices and hollows along the side of the path. An obvious example of this is a small, flat area to the R of the path which is host to a profusion of wild mint; the bees are strongly attracted to the purple-blue flowers and the herb's scent can be quite pungent, depending on the time of year.

The path continues easily, and after several hundred paces descends into a tiny bay known as Pwll Arian. To the R of this is an extensive area of long, lush grass feasting on the small streams that flow beneath your feet to the sea nearby. Consequently, the area is quite boggy and wet, expecially away from the path. Take some time to admire this bay: although there is no sand and in its place the rocks plunge aggressively into the sea, the small area has a particular rugged beauty due to the contrast of the serrated rocks beneath the emerald foam-topped waves.

From the small bay of Pwll Arian, the path climbs a short distance up an easy scramble of dust and sand to a cairn. It continues to be reasonably straight and well-defined, divided occasionally by P-stiles as it heads NE. Along this section fantastic views of the Strumble Head lighthouse are possible, together with the trail of neighbouring small islands: Carreg Onnen, Ynys Onnen and Ynys Meicel. These stand out distinctly from the surrounding swell and the peace is only broken slightly by the occasional blink from the lighthouse. You might also see the car ferry or catamaran ploughing its way from Fishguard to Ireland beyond the lighthouse and its band of rocks and islands. The view improves even further as you progress NE, although you do have to take care with a few deep gullies and narrow sections of the path as you

131

continue. You will make quick progress along this section of the Coastal Path and will soon be clambering your way along the route just in front of the lighthouse, where you will meet a couple more P-stiles and need to cross a treaded footbridge.

From the footbridge the path follows a furrow of gorse as it traverses NE along the slope opposite the lighthouse. This section ends in a P-stile over a fence, which then connects you with a tarmac track that services the lighthouse. Eventually, after a few hundred paces, the path leaves the tarmac (which leads off S), and the first views of the N coastline of Pembrokeshire come into view as you come over a slight rise. These are very impressive and extend for a considerable distance towards the harbour at Fishguard. There are a few more P-stiles to cope with, but the walking is easy and enjoyable.

There are several idyllic bays along this N stretch of the Coastal Path, namely Pwll Bach, Pwllong and Porthsychan. The path meanders up and down, in and out of these bays, sometimes descending high above dark caves and at other almost swamped by tall ferns and brambles. Here and there are the occasional trumpet flowers of the sea bindweed, and there are numerous P-stiles with waymarkers to guide you. You should keep to the designated Coastal Path for about 2km (1¼ miles) more.

The first two bays are observed from high above on the cliff-tops, where the path hangs precariously. Although descending to the small stretches of sand in the bays might be possible it is not necessary, since this is much easier in the following bay of Porthsychan. You might see some brave sea anglers belayed from the rocks near the immense swell in these bays, but they are usually very well camouflaged!

Before Porthsychan, the path trails briefly around the small peninsula of Trwyn Llwyd before descending decisively into a leafy glade of tall ferns and rich grasses. There are numerous wild flowers along this section, including the bright yellow ragwort. Once again, there are a few P-stiles, and some small tributaries are crossed via an assortment of makeshift footbridges before you reach the small beach in Porthsychan. This bay is a very restful place. There is a small sand dune that is an ideal place from which to look out to sea, and

the beach is scattered with seaweed and debris from the small fishing vessels in the area. When the author last visited the bay he was fortunate enough to see a lively group of young seals basking in the sunshine as they bobbed around a short distance out to sea. Like the anglers, they blend in with the crashing waves perfectly and take some patience to spot!

The way past Garn Gilfach and back to Garn Fawr
Allow 1½ hours

From Porthsychan you should continue NE along the Coastal Path as it climbs out of the bay into a section of open land. This is a refreshing contrast to the narrow cliff-top route and you are soon back into thick gorse again. There is an abundance of common ragwort and tall thistles and you will need to cross a few brooks, together with a few more obligatory P-stiles. The open scrubland develops into cattle grazing and the path continues to climb, remaining close to the coast. The gradient relents after a few hundred paces and after this the path settles down to its more acceptable undulating manner.

After a few hundred paces more you should be able to spot a distinctive white cottage ahead, and a short distance further on the path changes direction to head SE along the side of a narrow bay. You will reach a crossroads of two paths, one being the Coastal Path which continues NE and the other an inland path heading SE. You should turn R, off the Coastal Path and follow the latter; there is a worn waymarker at this stage (MR 913407) to assist you.

The new path is clear and good, and leads you into an area of slightly inclined sheep pasture. As you progress you will need to cross a fence via a P-stile, and the path then changes to a twin track that has been used by vehicles. The route continues to climb and there is a wiggle in the path, after which the track is made up mainly of loose rubble. You will pass close by the white cottage of Penrhyn, noticed earlier, which is in a delightful position affording great views down the narrow gully to the tiny bay and the deep swell beyond. The path adopts the 'grass-down-the-middle' characteristic and there is dense bracken on both sides. You will then enter the National Trust region of Good Hope, as indicated by a sign along the way.

Pass through a large metal gate immediately after the National Trust sign, after which trees encroach on to the gravel path. There are also more clumps of brambles and their heavy blossom or fruit, in season. Next you will pass a sharp fork to the L, which should be disregarded, and the relentless climb continues as you head further inland, due s. There are occasional waymarkers in the reverse direction, indicating the way to the Coastal Path. After about 1km (⅝ mile) you will reach a tarmac road, on to which you should turn L.

Be particularly vigilant on the road, since you need to leave it after only 100 paces or so at a small settlement called Trenewydd on the R. There is a wide gate to go through, which leads to a driveway with a large house to the L. Since this is a private drive as well as a right of way, be sure to close the gate behind you. The path continues across the brief patch of tarmac to the R of the house and soon climbs into sparse woodland. An enclosed narrow lane bordered by blackberries on either side develops quickly and climbs for several hundred paces. To the R, looking ahead, you will soon be able to see the distinctive crags of Garn Gilfach and Garn Folch.

After a few hundred paces, you will reach a T-junction close to the crags (MR 912393), where you should turn R. The path now changes into a sandy trail that follows a contour due w. This flat section traverses the rocky outcrops to the s and passes through areas of scattered bracken; there are good views to the N of the now familiar coastline. This section of the route is particularly gentle, quiet and peaceful.

After a few hundred paces you will pass through a loose metal gate and the path turns to head s for a few metres. There are now pleasant views of both prominent outcrops: Garn Gilfach to the SE and Garn Fawr to the WSW. The path subsequently turns R to continue its trek w towards the sunset. Take care while walking this sweeping N slope, since there is an array of paths in all directions. You should head due W and surrender little height until quite close to Garn Fawr. The flat terrain is covered with bracken and the route follows a deep trench

between ferns, while the lighthouse stands by to the N. Finally, the path descends a slight slope to meet up with a tarmac road. Here you should turn L and head uphill: this final climb is deceptive! Within 500 paces or so you will pass over the rise of the road and the car park is a short distance further on to the R. If you are fortunate enough to tackle this route on a fine, sunny day it is well worth the walk back up to the top of Garn Fawr to watch the sunset.

Alternative routes

ESCAPES

There are several possible short cuts along this route, taken simply by leaving the Coastal Path earlier than recommended. For example, when you reach the beautiful bay of Porthsychan you could leave by the inland path that heads sw. Eventually this joins another heading due w, which leads to the small settlement of Tydraw. You can pick up the tarmac road here and should follow it due s up the long hill back to the car park. This road is quiet, but the views and general scenery are not as pleasant as on the complete tour.

EXTENSIONS

This walk can be lengthened easily, since you can proceed further along the coast and take another inland path. From Penrhyn, you may wish to continue E as far as Carregwastad Point, which is reputed to be the place where, in 1797, the French Black Legion landed with aspirations of marching to Chester and Liverpool. However, they surrendered without bloodshed to the local Home Guard from Llanwnda. There are various myths surrounding the surrender, including one account in which the invading forces mistook the scarlet dresses of the wives of Llanwnda for a mighty force and consequently believed that they were outnumbered. To continue the walk from this point, you should return via the sw path to the old farmhouse at Tre-Howel, where you join the tarmac road. Walking about 500 paces w along this leads to Trenewydd (MR 913397), where you can continue along the recommended return route.

Route 18: THE PRESELI HILLS

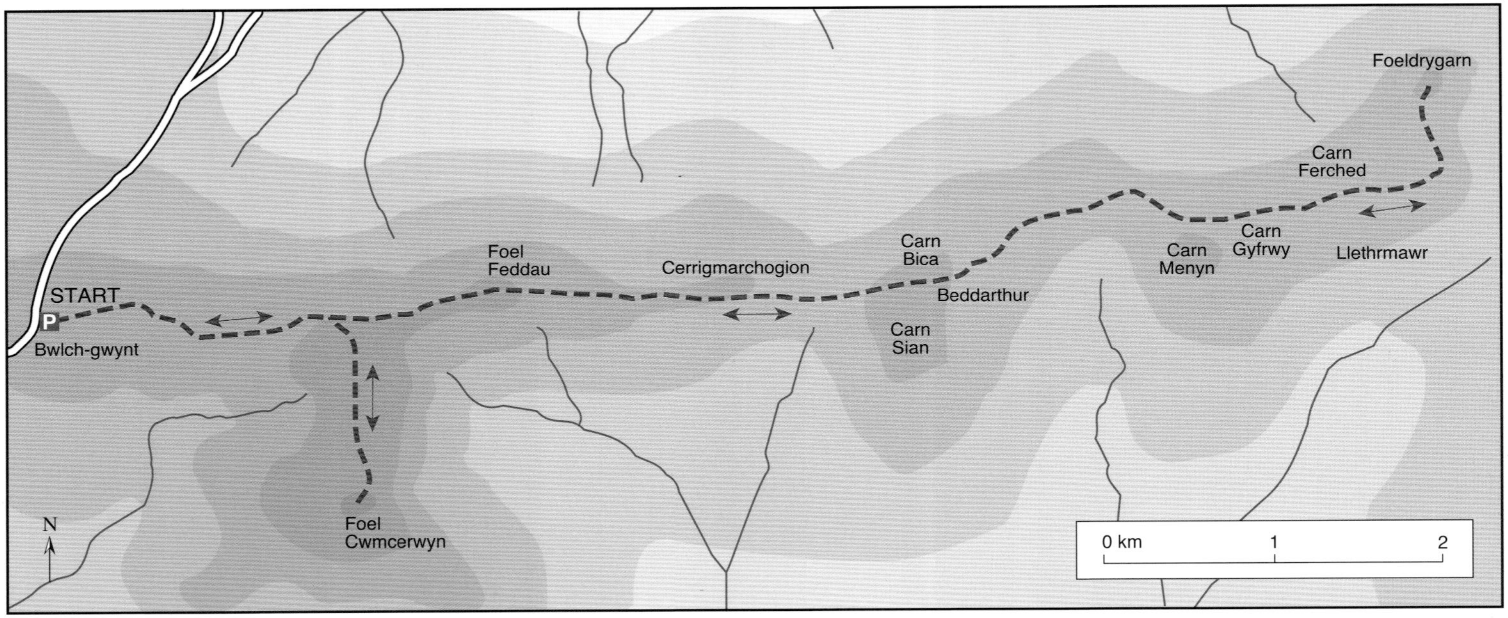

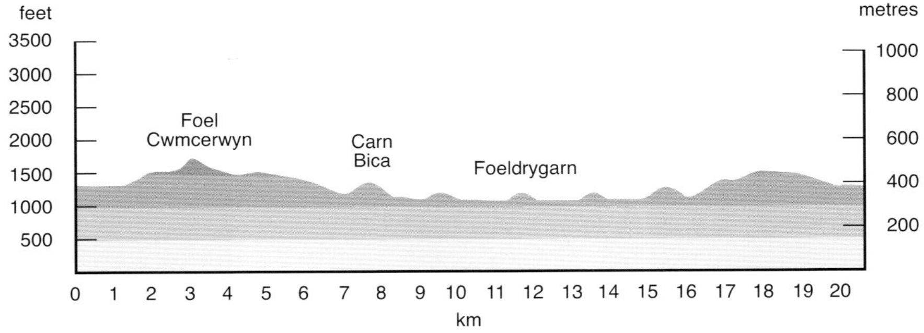

Foeldrygarn

Carn
Ferched

Carn
Gyfrwy

Llethrmawr

Carn
Menyn

Carn
Bica

Beddarthur

Carn
Sian

Cerrigmarchogion

Foel
Feddau

Foel
Cwmcerwyn

START

P

Bwlch-gwynt

N

0 km   1   2

feet

3500
3000
2500
2000
1500
1000
500

metres

1000
800
600
400
200

Foel
Cwmcerwyn

Carn
Bica

Foeldrygarn

0 1 2 3 4 5 6 7 8 9 10 11 12 13 14 15 16 17 18 19 20
km

Route 18 • The Preseli Hills

STARTING LOCATION
Car park at Bwlch-gwynt.
OLM 35/MR 075323.
Capacity for 20 cars .
No toilets.

ALTERNATIVE STARTING LOCATION
None.

PUBLIC TRANSPORT
None.

OVERVIEW/INTEREST
Linear walk along the Mynydd Preseli of inland
   Pembrokeshire.
Vast ridge walking across rolling hills.
Visit King Arthur's grave and the Neolithic fort of
   Foeldrygarn, and passes numerous Neolithic
   burial sites.

FOOTPATHS
Paths are indistinct in places, waymarking is
   sparse and a compass is essential.
Terrain is wet and boggy.
Thick heather and stubble can restrict the pace.

GRADING   Moderate
TIME ALLOWANCE   6½ hours
DISTANCE
Excluding height   20km (12.5 miles)
TOTAL HEIGHT GAINED   429m (1,407ft)
PRINCIPAL HEIGHTS
Foel Cwmcerwyn 536m (1,759ft)
Foel Feddau 467m (1,533ft)
Foeldrygarn 363m (1,191ft)

The way to Foel Cwmcerwyn _Allow 1½ hours_

The Preseli Hills dominate the higher ground in the
N of Pembrokeshire and comprise an extensive,
rolling ridge with many cwms and valleys
descending to both the N and s. The scenery is
unique, not only in comparison with the coast
further s, but also when set against the harsh
terrain of North Wales or the more aesthetic
Cumbrian Hills. The sparse landscape, occasionally
interrupted by jagged outcrops and ancient
settlements, is isolated and unspoilt and is worth
further exploration.

This walk starts from the small high-level car
park at Bwlch-gwynt, just off the B4329, to the E of
Cerrig Lladron. The car park is really just a worn
grassy area, rutted through use and muddy in
places. There is a wire fence to the s, forming the
boundary of a cattle field, while the N side is an
open, sweeping hillside providing beautiful views
towards Cardigan. You should walk away from the
road, heading due E, with the fence to your R.
There is a gradual incline and the grass is uneven.
However, the path is wide and clear and the
summit of Foel Cwmcerwyn can be seen for a short
while to the SE. Soon coniferous woodland extends
to the R beyond the fence, and the path becomes
more sheltered.

After a few hundred paces you will reach the
corner of the forestry area after which it recedes
away from the path. In deviating from the forest,
the route heads SE across open grassland, down a
slight slope. In this area the terrain can be very wet
and marshy, since the rainfall collects near to the
saddle of Bwlch Pennant that lies ahead. There is a
combination of heather, reeds and marsh grasses
and the slopes begin to fall away to the L, speckled
with occasional hardy sheep. After a few hundred
paces the path joins the forest once more and
follows the boundary fence. Continue due E up the
steeper slope. As you climb the ground will become
firmer and drier, and you will soon reach the edge
of the forest, where the path divides. At this
position (MR 092323) a view of the Preseli Hills
opens up for the first time due to the sudden
reduction in gradient. The ridge is a very wide
plateau high above the villages of Eglwyswrw and
Blaenffos and is particularly bleak in poor visibility.

To the E the wide, rutted track proceeds down the undulating carpet of grass and occasional crags to Foeldrygarn; to the SE a fainter path heads uphill towards Foel Cwmcerwyn. You should take the latter if the weather is good, since the views from the top are worth the effort. Although the path begins in a very indistinct state, climbing a grassy slope very close to the forestry boundary, it soon develops into a comfortable track. After a couple of hundred paces it changes course at an inscribed limestone post to head due S, and then continues fairly straight for about 1km (⅝ mile). The gradient is not severe, but is enough to sap some of your strength! While on the climb, most of the surrounding panorama is obscured by the immediate moorland. After about 500m (542yd) you will come over a rise from which you will be able to see the summit ahead, still a fair distance away. Better views will begin to develop to the R towards Foel Eryr in the W. You will need to cross more heather and scrub before reaching the summit of Foel Cwmcerwyn.

The summit is marked by a cairn and triangulation point. There are pleasant views down a deep cwm to the E, looking across to the flat spur that is crowned by an assortment of cairns and outcrops, near to Beddarthur. Looking to the SE there is the characteristic patchwork farmland of Pembrokeshire, with the occasional coniferous woodland.

The way to Beddarthur and on to Foeldrygarn

Allow 3 hours

From the summit of Foel Cwmcerwyn it is best to retrace your steps, due N, to the ridge path. This may seem odd since from the map it would appear easy to cut the corner and join the path further along the ridge. However, the terrain changes to the E of Foel Cwmcerwyn such that the slope steepens greatly and the grassland becomes very uneven and wet, so the apparent short cut can become unpleasant and difficult. There is also a fence to be crossed near to the ridge.

Back on the ridge there are two paths and the choice matters little, since they join each other further on. However, the most N is recommended since it follows the high-level route and includes Foel Feddau – a small, grassy peak with a cairn – about 500m (542yd) along the ridge. It is worthwhile gazing down the vast slope to Carnau Lladron, where buzzards swoop and play in summer.

The slight incline up to Foel Feddau is rewarded by a long, steady descent across Cerrigmarchogion. The walking is very each in this region, as the scrubland relents and the path is wide and clear. It continues due E and there is a collection of small crags to the R. The terrain appears to be flat but, in general, you are losing height – this will become painfully apparent on the return route! You will pass through sections of glacial debris in the form of huge dolerite stacks reputed to be the petrified knights of King Arthur, and the path weaves in and out of these ghostly outcrops. After several hundred paces and a gentle descent to the shallow saddle between Mynydd-bach (to the W) and the larger Carn Siân (to the SE), you will approach an unclear crossroads. The saddle is usually wet and is covered in thick marsh grass. You should disregard the paths leaving to the NE and due S, and continue due E up the incline ahead. To the NE you will be able to see the skeletal outcrop of Carn Goedog, while ahead are the outcrops of Carn Bica and Carn Siân.

Soon after you begin to cross the boggy saddle you will be able to follow distinct white waymarker posts that assist navigation across the poor terrain and on up the slope ahead. These should be followed, since the W side of Carn Siân is feature-less and confusing, especially in bad visibility. The path climbs quickly, passing in-between Carn Bica and Carn Siân, and when it starts to descend again, you will see the feature of Beddarthur a short distance ahead. This comprises a neat, oval ring of rocks that are said to mark the burial place of King Arthur. However, since there are many such reputed sites throughout the UK, it may be one of the many Neolithic burial mounds found in the Preseli Hills area. From Beddarthur, the ground sweeps away towards the large rocky area of Carn Menyn to the E, and the more distant Foeldrygarn to the ENE. The paths divide in a confusing aray at Beddarthur and you should head ESE, keeping to the high ground. The path can become unclear, so study your compass bearing if in doubt.

The terrain changes gradually now, from the hardy grass of the previous sections of the walk to thick, clumped heather. In places the ground is very rutted and uneven due to farm vehicle use. After several hundred paces, the route begins to climb again to the L of some more crags: Carn Menyn and Carn Gyfrwy. Particular aspects of these resemble outcrops of North Wales, such as Castell y Gwynt in the Glyderau. As you progress amid this isolated and desolate landscape of sweeping plains and jagged rocks, you will be able to see a tall transmission mast that is SW of your current position (MR 141327). This is the television mast that lies just outside Gwarllwyn Wood. Ahead, the characteristic summit of Foeldrygarn becomes clearer amid the expansive views of the E.

Beddarthur deep within the Preseli Hills.

In summer and early autumn the E area of the Preseli Hills is a rich combination of delicate pastel shades. The grass supports many shades of green and yellow while the virulent heather adds a wonderful rich, contrasting purple. Following the path E, you will soon reach the coniferous forest of Llethrmawr S of Carn Ferched. The path tracks close to the whole length of the N edge of the forest. Foeldrygarn lies to the NE as you follow the boundary of the wood. Do not be tempted to cut across the scrubland to the NE, as the path is well defined and follows a good, clear route if you are patient. Just beyond the E end of the forest the path swings around to head due N, heading away from the trees and directly for the summit of Foeldrygarn. The intermediate scrubland is rough and will restrict your progress if attempted – allow the path to help you.

Foeldrygarn, the Hill with Three Cairns, is thought to be the remains of an Iron Age hill fort, complete with a system of ramparts. There are also three distinct Bronze Age burial mounds along the summit ridge. Although not very noticeable at close quarters, aerial studies have revealed a fine dimpling effect across the summit, indicating the presence of over 200 hut circles on the summit. You will find that the track across the preceding land is easy until the gradient increases suddenly and you need to climb through the embankments and natural rock features of the s slope. There are several sheer outcrops before you reach the rock-strewn summit cairns, and the heather persists almost to the summit triangulation point. This quiet, historical place is worth a few minutes' rest and appreciation.

The way back to Bwlch-gwynt *Allow 2 hours*

Once you have hopped between the three summit cairns of Foeldrygarn and savoured the panoramic views of inland Pembrokeshire, you should retrace your steps w. Although navigation is assisted by the altitude, you will find it is easiest to return by the route used for the ascent; even though a path is shown to head sw on the map, it is best to head due s for about 500m (542yd) until you pick up the path near the forest once again.

The return route is not easy. Since the w end of the Preseli Hills is considerably higher than the E, there is a net climb required for the second half of the walk. In addition, there are numerous small rises such as Carn Ferched, Beddarthur and Cerrigmarchogion along the way, and these will test tired legs relentlessly. However, the nature of the Preseli Hills is such that the views on the return are refreshing and the perspectives different, and you may have the good fortune to find that previously poor visibility has improved for the return trip. As you trudge your way w, up the wide, grassy slopes, do not become complacent about your bearing, since the terrain can appear very different and you could easily wander off-course and incur large detours. Once you have reached the forest of Llethrmawr you should head due w for the duration of the return route, with occasional deviations to accommodate the gentle rises and descents. The return route is about 9km (5½ miles) long and much of it is uphill. This makes the final view of the car park very rewarding indeed!

Alternative routes

ESCAPES
This linear walk is long and can be impeded severely when the weather is bad. In order to shorten the walk, you should simply retrace your steps back to the car park at any point along the outward route. Any apparently attractive descents N or S from the main ridge will incur long diversions aross difficult, waterlogged ground.

EXTENSIONS
No extensions are recommended other than the minor diversions mentioned in the main route.

Delicate heathers on the lower slopes of Foeldrygarn.

Route 19: ST DAVID'S AND THE RAMSEY SOUND

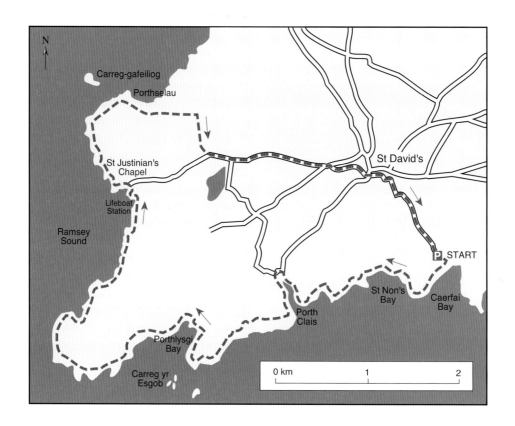

Carreg-gafeiliog
Porthselau
St Justinian's Chapel
Lifeboat Station
Ramsey Sound
St David's
START
P
St Non's Bay
Caerfai Bay
Porth Clais
Porthlysgi Bay
Carreg yr Esgob

0 km   1   2

N

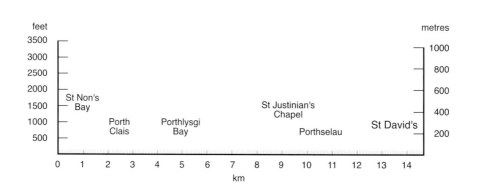

feet   metres

3500
                                                                        1000
3000
2500   800
2000
                                                                        600
1500   St Non's   St Justinian's
        Bay   Chapel   400
1000   Porth   Porthlysgi
        Clais   Bay   Porthselau   St David's   200
500

     0 1 2 3 4 5 6 7 8 9 10 11 12 13 14
                            km

Route 19 • St David's and the Ramsey Sound

STARTING LOCATION
Car park at Caerfai Bay.
OLM 35/MR 759244.
Capacity for 30 cars .
No toilets.

ALTERNATIVE STARTING LOCATION
None.

PUBLIC TRANSPORT
None.

OVERVIEW/INTEREST
Fascinating coastal and inland walk, with
  abundant seals and birdlife on the coastal
  sections.
Passes by Ramsey Island and the Ramsey Sound,
  and offers views of Whitesands Bay.
Detours possible to explore the wonderful beach
  at Caerfai Bay and the cathedral in the city of
  St David's.
Features include St Non's Chapel and Well, Porth
  Clais and relics of the lime industry, the
  Lifeboat Station and St Justinian's chapel.

FOOTPATHS
Paths are clear throughout.
Coastal sections are dangerous and exposed in
  places.
Parts of the route pass through busy streets and
  along narrow roads.
Terrain is varied.

GRADING   Moderate
TIME ALLOWANCE   5 hours
DISTANCE
Excluding height   15.5km (9.7 miles)
TOTAL HEIGHT GAINED   50m (164ft)
PRINCIPAL HEIGHTS
None

The way to Porth Clais   *Allow 1 hour*

The car park at Caerfai Bay could not be much
nearer the sea. It is made up of sandy rubble and
slopes away towards the cliff-tops with the sea far
below you. To the SE the glorious sands of Caerfai
Bay tempt you to venture down to them; leave
yourself enough time to bathe your feet after the
walk, as this is strongly recommended!

The Coastal Path runs along the S edge of the car
park, a few metres away. It is slightly lower than
the level of the car park beyond a bench, and there
is a brief descent over worn steps to reach it. Once
there, turn R and head off SW. The path is the usual
compacted sand found in this area and is bordered
by ferns and scrubland. The views of Caerfai Bay
improve as you progress along the cliff-tops and
across the ocean, to the S, you can often see the
industrial plants beyond the wide stretch of sea
called St Brides Bay.

There are a few national park waymarkers
indicating the route of the Coastal Path, and after
a short distance a wooden railing guards walkers
from the sheer drops to the L. This is a particular
feature of the coastal sections of this route. There
are many places where the drops are very severe.
These are not signed or fenced off, so be careful
and restrain youngsters, as the benign appearance
of this pretty seaside walk can obscure some
potentially fatal hazards.

As you continue, the island of Penpleidiau, at the
end of the small peninsula to the E, comes into view.
Soon after this the path turns suddenly to the N,
following the coastline. For a while the path then
drifts slightly inland and there are several campsites
nearby. The make-up of the path changes from
dusty sand to the damper ground of stagnant brooks.
You are now entering St Non's Bay, which is much
more rocky and disordered than Caerfai Bay. There
are several deep gullies leading down to the crashing
waves below and the path undulates gently ahead,
remaining in view for a considerable distance.

St Non's Bay is so called because a few hundred metres inland of the Coastal Path is the ancient monument of St Non's Chapel. The derelict chapel and ancient well are located in pleasant surroundings amid gorse and wild flowers. This place is reputed to be the birthplace of St David, who is said to have been born in a violent thunderstorm around AD 520. The chapel was built in dedication later, only to fall into ruin following the Reformation. The well is possibly pre-Christian in origin, having been adopted later by the Catholics, and is reputed to be a curing source for eye ailments. Any path leaving to the R, heading inland from St Non's Bay, will serve the chapel ruins and you should return by the same route to the Coastal Path.

The path continues through a variety of terrain, from thick hedgerows of gorse, ferns and heather to open and exposed cliff-tops that peer down on to secluded bays and tiny beaches. There are plateaux and contrasting rugged sections, but in general the terrain is flatter than elsewhere along the coast. After several hundred metres of beautiful coastline the path leaves the shelter of dense ferns and heads NW, following the E side of a long bay. This gradually develops into a tiny harbour, with small fishing vessels glinting in the sun as they ride the incoming swell. This is Porth Clais.

Porth Clais is a long, natural creek with a pebbly slipway leading to a man-made, concrete section. There is no beach, but the small harbour is a delightful place to visit as an excursion from St David's, which lies 1km (⅝ mile) to the NE. There is a great deal of history attached to Porth Clais, which becomes obvious as you descend towards the concrete harbour surround through a group of tall trees. The harbour is one of many in Pembrokeshire that served several lime kilns; there are the relics of five kilns here. From the mid-seventeenth century to around 1900 Pembrokshire was an important agricultural provider of cereals, specifically wheat and oats. To maximize yields, the acidic soils were treated with lime. However, lime was too hazardous to transport, due to its vigorous reaction with water, so the raw products of limestone and coal were transported by boat from nearby and burnt close to where the boats landed.

Porth Clais is almost perfectly designed for this purpose, its shallow slipway allowing the ships to beach easily and the reliable tracks heading inland ideal for the horse-drawn transportation of the lime to the fields and farms.

The traditional use of lime was eventually replaced by modern fertilizers and the industry rapidly went into decline. Now all that is left are the enigmatic stone-built hearths and kilns; usually covered with ivy, the rough-hewn crucibles overflow with brambles. There are several good examples on both sides of Porth Clais, and in some cases remnants of the limeburner's hovel remain adjacent to the kiln.

The way to Treginnis and the Ramsey Sound
Allow 1 hour

The Coastal Path climbs quite steeply out of the harbour on the W side, amid tall hedges of fern and whitethorn and well above the obsolete lime kilns. After a few hundred paces the terrain opens out again and you will pass a cream-coloured cottage on the R. There are several rickety P-stiles and refreshing views become possible of the N, specifically of the outcrop of Garn Fawr, near Strumble Head. The path continues as the beautiful coast unfolds. It is dusty and sandy, interspersed with clumps of grass. Ahead of you the S end of Ramsey Island soon appears, to the W.

The coast in this section is a varied scene of natural arches of rock and long, isolated peninsulas that are usually accompanied by small islands. This is particularly true in the region of Porthlysgi Bay, where the path descends to the pebbly shore and meanders through beached seaweed. In the centre of the bay is the island of Carreg yr Esgob. The venture along the beach is soon over, as the path climbs out of the bay to enter the area of Lower Treginnis, indicated by a National Trust sign nearby. There is also a fingerpost indicating a path leading off to St David's to the R; this should be disregarded as you continue along the Coastal Path.

The next section is of some contrast to the usual sand and dust, as it is boggy and must be crossed with the help of occasional stepping stones. The terrain changes to a more barren, almost mountainous type, with abundant heather and boulders in-between the frequent lumps of high ground. The path passes through a K-gate and climbs a short, rugged way to the top of one of the rises. There are several paths in and around the gorse across the subsequent plateau; you should continue w, changing gradually to NW, faithfully following the coastline as you proceed. In this region sight of the cliffs and shore is lost because of the comparatively high ground. However, this loss is more than compensated for by the complete view of Ramsey Island to the w. This becomes possible as you round the headland and begin to head due N 1km (⅝ mile) on from Porthlysgi Bay.

Ramsey Island is a rugged plateau of ancient farmland that is now owned by the RSPB and is a dedicated nature reserve. The Island of the Ram, as it is also known, boasts the two significant hills of Carn Llundain and Carn Ysgubor. Once there were also two chapels: one dedicated to St Justinian and the other to St Dyfanog. St Justinian is reputed to have retired to Ramsey due to disagreements with the mainland monks; to complete his exile, legend recalls that he cut the land connecting Ramsey to the coast, leaving behind the savage rocks in Ramsey Sound now known as The Bitches. Ramsey Sound is a formidable stretch of water with strong currents and tides. It is well worth taking one of the many boat trips to the island that run from Easter to October, as some of the scenery is absolutely spectacular; for example, the cliffs of the w side are among the highest in Pembrokeshire, and there is also a thriving seal colony. These features are complemented by some breathtaking caves and arches and a struggle back to shore through the currents around The Bitches.

The Penmaenmelyn peninsula is the furthest w point of mainland Wales, but is quite a modest landmark. Indeed, the stretch of narrow, sandy path is significant because of the copper mining history and not because of its location. As you progress N you are accompanied by the smooth,

The mighty cliffs of Ramsey Island.

fast-flowing waters of the Sound to the w and the path will approach a fenced area. This holds the remains of the Treginnis copper mine; there is a sign warning of the dangerous disused mineshafts in the small area near to the fence and you should take care.

Copper mining was an active industry for most of the nineteenth century, but the mines here were not worked with sophisticated machinery as in the search for the rich deposits in Cornwall. In Pembrokeshire, a mine was usually worked by a small number of men who blasted the ore from deep within the coastline and pulled it up in large buckets with winching machinery. The Treginnis mine operated until 1883, when a fatal accident invoked its closure. Today only the foundations of the small buildings associated with the mine and the ruins of some of the winch supports have survived the ruthless climate of the Ramsey Sound. The mineshafts remain, but are obscured by the vigorous brambles and heather that have adopted them.

The way to the Lifeboat Station and St Justinian's Chapel *Allow 1 hour*

From the disused mine the path continues N but winds eccentrically up short, steep sections of the route. There are exposed tree roots and rocks to watch out for along here. When you reach the plateau stage once more, the Coastal Path drifts to the NE as it faithfully follows the shores that are some distance below to the L. From this point (MR 717238) you will have superb views of the w coastline, which is decorated by the Lifeboat Station in the distance. This structure is distinctive due to its curved corrugated roof and the steep slipway leading to the water's edge. The view improves as you progress N.

You will pass several stiles of different types and further remnants of the copper mining era. There

The St David's Lifeboat Station at Porthstinian, looking towards Ramsey Island.

are patches of lush grass and ferns before you leave the National Trust area of Lower Treginnis, and the coastline continues to dominate the route; there is a rich combination of natural arches and small bays until you reach the Lifeboat Station, after just over 1km (⅝ mile). There are various picnic spots around the RNLI post and the station is a great place for a lengthy mid-route rest. The station is usually open to visitors and you can wander round the St David's Lifeboat and chat to some of the crew. The lifeboat first came to St David's in 1869, when industry thrived in the area and relied on the sea to transport the cereal crops, lime and coal around the treacherous coastline. Although the industrial use of the sea has waned over the last century, the RNLI still provide an essential service to the pleasure craft and small fishing vessels in the area.

The Lifeboat Station is also the place where the tours of Ramsey Island begin, should you wish to take one of these another time. In addition, at the top of the steep pathway to the station you will find the remains of St Justinian's Chapel. This relic stands in private grounds but it can be viewed remarkably well from the path, completing a particularly interesting section of the route.

The way to St David's and back to Caerfai Bay

Allow 2 hours

The Coastal Path continues near to the tour reservation cabins and crosses over the cabling of the slipway system, to enter an exposed area of the cliffs. This quickly becomes fenced on both sides, so that you are following a narrow channel which has suffered extreme erosion in places. Once you have climbed out of Porthstinian, where the Lifeboat Station is located, views unfold to the NW of the popular beaches of Whitesands Bay. The path improves and after a few hundred paces it becomes very wide, while the array of small peninsulas and bays continues to the L.

The route passes several waymarkers and stiles and you should continue to follow the Coastal Path. The terrain changes slightly along this final section of the coast, as the path follows around the edge of several grassy fields and meadows and is a twin track in parts. Out at sea, to the NW, you will see the disordered, partly submerged clump of rocks of Carreg-gafeiliog. The Coastal Path now meanders to the E.

After a few hundred paces the path begins to head ESE and approaches the bay of Porthselau, the most S part of the Whitesands Bay area. You will pass a large campsite to the R, where the tents seem to hang over the dunes to the R of the path. Just beyond this point (MR 726259) you should turn R to head inland, walking due E. The terrain changes greatly as the path climbs away from the coast. There is a deep groove surrounded by lush vegetation and there are also some waymarkers hidden among the grass. Take care to check your bearing, as there is another path that heads SE. The correct route continues L, due E, over a couple of stiles to reach a grassy field. The path then follows around the edge of this and develops into a twin track with electric fences to either side. The gradient remains uphill but eases greatly, the route being guided by yellow waymarkers. After about 400 paces through several fields and meadows, heading due E, the path reaches a large metal gate, after which you should turn R. The path changes to a tarmac track and turns through the farmyards of Treleddyn Farm. You will now be heading due S.

The path continues S for about 500m (542yd), passing a few ponds to the R before ending at a T-junction with a wider, more established tarmac road. Here you should turn L and follow this quiet coastal route due E into the city of St David's. This is a lengthy section of almost 2km (1¼ miles) and you might be accompanied by other pedestrians returning from the Lifeboat Station or one of the many Ramsey Island tours. There are wild trailing toadflax in the hedgerows along the roadside.

After 1km (⅝ mile) the road is joined by another to the R, and a few hundred paces further on you should fork left for the city. This route brings you into St David's via a large car park to the R of the road, just short of the city itself. St David's is situated on a hill and the tarmac road climbs steeply; if you peep over the tall stone wall on the L you can sneak pleasant views of the cathedral. This is an appealing combination of architecture from many periods, dating from 1176. In particular, there were numerous additions throughout the Middle Ages. There are idiosyncratic qualities to the construction too: the floor slopes upwards and the columns lean outwards. There is a great deal of history and interest surrounding the cathedral and it is recommended for a prolonged visit. In the summer there are often choral concerts and organ recitals that are also worth attending. For pleasant evening strolls, the grounds of the cathedral, the Close and the Bishop's Palace are worth investigating further.

The city of St David's is not large and, as yet, is not unduly spoiled by tourism. The route follows the long hill into the city square, passing several good pubs and restaurants. There are a number of souvenir shops and craft stores, but in general St David's retains its great character and is usually calm, unhurried and romantic.

Shortly before you reach the Cross Square in the centre of the city (you may wish to return to this point after exploring St David's in more detail), you should turn R opposite the Tabernacle in Goat Street (MR 753253) to walk due s along Stephens Lane. At the subsequent T-junction you should turn L and then take the first R, heading s once more. This brief residential section of the walk ends quickly, with a footpath at the end of the lane that is waymarked for Caerfai Bay, Bryn-y-Garn and St David's. This gravel path runs along the rear of a few houses and a school before heading off SE into tall hedges of gorse.

After a few hundred paces the footpath ends with a skewed T-junction on another narrow coastal road. Here you should turn R on to a road that you will recognize as the approach road for the car park at Caerfai Bay, It descends gradually towards the coast, heading SE, past several pleasant cottages and dwellings and the occasional campsite. You will reach the car park after about 0.5km (⅓ mile). Do spend some time at Caerfai Bay if possible – reached by descending the many steps to the beach that begin a short distance to the E of the car park – as this is to be strongly recommended.

Alternative routes

ESCAPES

As with many of the coastal routes found in Pembrokeshire, this can conveniently be shortened to make it more suitable for evening strolls or half-day walks. For example, there are many inland roads and footpaths from the more popular bays; a suitable route is to proceed to the small harbour at Porth Clais and head inland from here along the tarmac road that serves the harbour, into St David's. This reaches Goat Street near to the city car park, where the return route begins. A similar escape route can be made further along the coast by heading inland from the Lifeboat Station, close to St Justinian's Chapel.

EXTENSIONS

No extensions to this walk are recommended, as there is so much of interest along the main route. Time should be allowed to explore the cathedral in St David's and the delights of Caerfai Bay.

Dramatic fissures and gullies abound along the Pembrokeshire Coast.

147

Route 20: MARLOES AND ST BRIDES

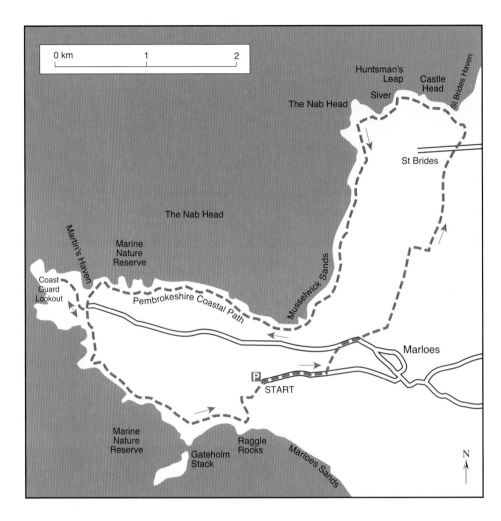

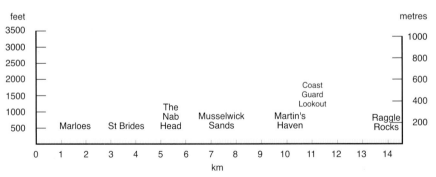

Route 20 • Marloes and St Brides

STARTING LOCATION
Large National Trust car park (usual charge).
OLM 36/MR 778083.
No toilets.

ALTERNATIVE STARTING LOCATION
Marloes village MR 789086.

PUBLIC TRANSPORT
Bus route Haverfordwest–Marloes (along the
    B4327 road).

OVERVIEW/INTEREST
Beautiful coastal walking near Skomer Marine
    Nature Reserve.
Many fantastic bays, cliffs and inlets, and the
    beaches at Marloes and Musselwick Sands.
Rich variety of flora and fauna.
Features include St Brides church and the Coast
    Guard Lookout.

FOOTPATHS
Paths are well defined and much of the route is
    clearly waymarked.
Narrow, eroded sections require great care and
    inland stretches need thought.
Terrain is mainly dry and free from mud.

GRADING   Easy
TIME ALLOWANCE   5½ hours
DISTANCE
Excluding height   14.5km (9.1 miles)
TOTAL HEIGHT GAINED   120m (394ft)
PRINCIPAL HEIGHTS
None

The way to St Brides church   *Allow 1½ hours*

Leave the large National Trust car park at the s exit, passing a collection box and a tourist map of the Marloes area as you proceed. This car park is the main one for the beautiful beaches of Marloes Sands and, although extensive, can be busy in high season. On the tarmac road that services the car park, turn L to head due E. This road is little more than a metalled track and is bordered by delicate, grassy hedges and a light covering of blown sand from the coast nearby. It climbs a slight slope as you proceed inland and there is an assortment of wild flowers in the hedgerows; in particular, look out for the sea bindweed with its pretty pink trumpet-flowers and trailing stems. In summer, there are many butterflies along this lane too.

After a few hundred paces of very easy walking you will pass the large farm complex at Marloes Court on the R. Just after these buildings there is a waymarker on the R of the road indicating a path leaving to the L, which you should take. A stepped P-stile marks the beginning of this path across open country. The first stile is quickly followed by a second as you pass through open pastures; the path follows to the R of the field, close to a wire fence. From the next P-stile it is possible to see the sea to the L, beyond the fields. A few paces further on you will need to cross another stepped P-stile, which leads to a second secluded coastal lane, just w of Marloes village. There is another waymarker and you should proceed to the R (due E) towards the village centre. Be sure to look out for the wild flowers that can be found on the outskirts of the village. You will pass a few large clumps of fuchsias and hydrangeas at which you should turn L, past a bench. The footpath continues across a crossroads and is waymarked efficiently. Within a few paces the tarmac changes to an established, wide gravel path that is bordered by very tall ferns. You are now heading ENE.

The gravel continues for a few hundred paces before gradually changing to a covering of red sand. The path also changes direction to head NNE and you will then pass The Old School to the L. The correct path continues to the R of the school, through a K-gate leading into a cornfield. The fork to the R at this position (MR 794088) should be disregarded.

The ease with which you tackle the next section of the walk depends on the season – whether there is tall wheat or stubble in the fields. In any case, the path follows the perimeter of the field and does not cross it, heading NE as indicated on the map. The path is clear and well waymarked to the L of the field. You will need to take care with the virulent brambles and nettles that border the path, especially if you favour shorts in summer!

The path follows the field faithfully, just E of due N, for a short distance before reaching another P-stile. From here there are good views of the coast, beyond the fields. After crossing another short section of stubble you need to pass through a rusty iron K-gate. A short distance beyond this a path leaves to the L over a stile, which should be disregarded. Follow the path around the field to the ESE. In the height of summer there will be a host of accompanying crickets in the wheat and corn here. Thankfully the ancient hedgerows have been retained and comprise a tangled mass of gorse and wild roses.

You should make good progress over the predominantly flat land and will pass a horse trough to the L, possibly complete with a few inquisitive equines! A short distance after this you will reach a P-stile to the R of a metal gate, which you should cross. This leads to the crossroads of a tarmac lane where you should turn L, to head NNE once more. This lane descends gently among hedgerows of honeysuckle, brambles and ferns and lasts for about 300 paces before it turns sharp L. Here (MR 799098) you should ignore the route to the L and continue N, over a P-stile and to the L of a large, round gatepost. There are waymarkers here to help.

Beyond the unusual round gatepost a meadow opens up ahead, to the L of a dense woodland of deciduous trees. The path follows close to these and is sheltered by them. To the L the land rises to the W and there may be a few lazing cattle around. After a few paces, you will reach a stone-stepped stile, which gives way to another similar meadow with the trees continuing to the L, now with a few conifers among them. This succession of stiles and meadows repeats a few times for the next 500 paces or so, accompanied by the gradual descent to the coast.

Intricate stained-glass is just one of St Brides' many treasures.

The way down culminates at an iron K-gate, which leads across a farmer's driveway to another similar K-gate. After this the terrain changes slightly to undulating grassland, and you will now be heading NE. You will need to cross a placid stream close to a stone wall on the L, while ahead is the church of St Brides. This lies beyond a K-gate, a cattle grid and an area of tarmac; another brook is also crossed. The church of St Brides (MR 803108) is Celtic in origin and dates from the thirteenth century. It lies just to the S of a pretty bay of the same name. Indeed, the name of St Brides has been adopted by much of the surrounding area, including St Brides Green and St Brides Cross, in addition to the bay of St Brides Haven. The church was thoroughly restored in 1868 and it has many colourful stained-glass windows for such a small building. There are also some rather unusual candle holders along the length of the aisle. It is well worth venturing inside; a key can be obtained from Cliff Cottage (just N of the church to the E of St Brides Haven) if the church is locked.

The way to Musselwick Sands and Martin's Haven

Allow 2 hours

The path proceeds through the churchyard, where there are some interesting Celtic sandstone crosses among the other memorials. The path is waymarked and leaves the churchyard via an iron gate. It then enters a small picnic area via a gap in the wall, and there are superb views of St Brides Haven ahead. The path continues w, passing over a wooden footbridge on its way around the bay. It starts to follow a walled path with the sea to the R, and will pass a bench. There are good views of a distinctive castellated building to the sw. The path proceeds over a stile in the wall and you are finally at the much-loved Pembrokeshire coast. Be sure to notice the enormous old red sandstone cliffs that abound in this section of the Coastal Path, both nearby and across St Brides Haven near to Cliff Cottage. Even if there is only a slight swell, the swirling rock pools at the foot of several deep gullies along this section of the route will be very impressive. Of course, although this walk is suitable for children, it is important to remember the perils of steep cliffs and narrow, crumbling paths.

Occasionally, along this section of the walk you may notice more of the sea bindweed found in the early stages of the route. After a short climb from St Brides Haven the path flattens out considerably and the walking is very pleasant indeed. The wall to the L rises to a height of almost 2m (6½ft), while the path remains sandy and clear. There are many deep and intrusive bays to the R beyond the flat cliff-tops, on which there is a tangled border of brambles. Orientation should be easy from now on, since you merely follow the Coastal Path for much of the remaining route. Be sure to disregard any stiles in the wall to the L for the next few kilometres, unless required by the Coastal Path itself. This is indicated by clear National Park way-markers along the path.

After a few hundred paces the path passes the narrow peninsula of Castle Head and then heads inland, close to Huntsman's Leap and Siver. Since the path becomes narrow further on, these open, grassy areas provide good places to stop for a breather. After this the path continues close to the cliff-tops until it reaches The Nab Head where it ventures inland again, by approximately 500m. There are many lesser paths in this area that head off to explore the extent of the headland, but these are not recommended – only the Coastal Path is maintained by the National Park Authority and hence other paths can be dangerous. The Coastal Path finally leaves the company of the wall by way of a p-stile. A short distance further on, as you round The Nab Head, views of Skomer Island become possible, together with the w end of the headland. You will pass a broken (when the author last visited) waymarker and then cross a stone-stepped stile over a wall. The path has more shale on it in this section and is bordered by ferns and bracken. There are patches of long grass rife with lazing crickets and an ever-present view of jagged cliffs ahead, steeped in the sea like giant razors. There are several p-stiles as you progress and the gorse encroaches close enough to scratch your calves! The route tends to undulate more than earlier because the path is closer to the cliff-tops. After more than 1km (⅝ mile) walking through tall bracken, the narrow, sandy path reaches the idyllic beach of Musselwick Sands.

You will probably first spy Musselwick Sands through thick ferns and brambles. The beach lies far below the Coastal Path and falls into two main bays that are separated by the Black Cliff, which lies approximately half-way between them. The path reaches a crossroads that is waymarked R for Musselwick Sands, L for the village of Marloes. You should disregard both of these and continue straight on, following the sign for Martin's Haven, proceeding R along the top of the cliffs. It is possible to descend to the beach if you wish, but this entails a long haul up to regain the path.

The path continues amid tall ferns and runs around the back of subsequent bays. It becomes grassy in this area and undulates as before, climbing considerably in places. The rock type changes drastically in this area: looking to the E, you might notice how red sandstone changes suddenly to a short section of sedimentary rock, followed by a longer expanse of more distinctive igneous rock. You will cross a couple of p-stiles and enter a mixed terrain of very dense, tall vegetation and short,

151

rocky outcrops. After a few hundred paces you will pass a side path to the L, waymarked for a campsite, in a region where the path is channelled by thick brambles and ferns on both sides. There is also a lone elder tree in the hedgerow to the L, which in summer is loaded with a profusion of jet-black elderberries among the brambles. There are blackthorn bushes in this area, too.

The deep and beautiful waters around Marloes.

A few paces along the path there is a sign on the L denoting farm access, and some more P-stiles. There is a great deal of gorse which is usually draped in many spiders' webs. You will pass a National Trust sign indicating the boundary of the West Hook Farm region. Following this the path becomes wetter. After several hundred paces more you will arrive at the pretty bay of Martin's Haven. The path descends a few steps to the sands and then proceeds due s past some disused, rusty

winching machinery. There is also a notice about diving safety on the R. Martin's Haven is a small and beautiful bay – another jewel of the Pembrokeshire coast.

This stage of the path is wide and made up of gravel. It is probably used for taking small dinghies to the sea and is therefore clear and well maintained. After a few paces the path passes a small collection of buildings to the R, where there is a display about the Skomer Marine Nature Reserve that is worth visiting. However, before you rush into this be sure not to miss the inscribed stone in the wall on the R. This is thought to be a foundation stone from a Celtic church originating from between the seventh and ninth centuries. There is also an emergency telephone nearby.

The way to Marloes Sands   *Allow 2 hours*

A few paces further up the gradual incline from Martin's Haven the track turns R and enters the National Trust Deer Park (Skomer Marine Nature Reserve). A small stream flows to the L from under the wall and the path turns sharp L and proceeds up the grassy slope that follows, which is bordered by ferns. You will be able to view Stokholm Island over the wire fence to the SW. At this stage (MR 760090) you can leave the path, heading W for the Coast Guard Lookout on the peninsula. This is the highest point in the area: 50m (164ft)! This small extension is strongly recommended, since it provides superlative views of Skomer Island with its characteristic stack on the L.

After visiting the Coast Guard Lookout, you should continue due S along the Coastal Path. You will pass a National Trust sign for the Deer Park area, beyond which there are some of the most breathtaking views in Pembrokeshire: amid shimmering seas, Stokholm Island forms the background to the expanse of jagged rocks that comprise the W shores of the Marloes Peninsula. Take care when looking S, as the path is very worn in this area. There are some signs and small amounts of flimsy wire fencing; in places the path has crumbled into the sea, so be especially careful with young walkers.

As you progress S along the narrow path with its gorse verges, the view ahead continues to improve. There are many tall, jutting rows of rocks steeped in the blue-green waters of the shore, while further ahead you will soon be able to see Gateholm Island, which is a lengthy, truncated peninsula. It is also possible to look across the many bays and natural rocky waterbreaks to the golden beaches of Marloes Sands, which is where the route ventures next.

153

A view of the beautiful and unspoilt coastline near St Brides.

The path now improves and is predominantly flat and sandy, with some gravel and scrubland in-between. You may hear a few seagull calls, attracted by activity on the popular beaches nearby. You should make good progress along the path, and after several hundred paces will pass a stile that is waymarked for the local youth hostel at Runwayskiln. Disregard this and follow the Coastal Path; there is a profusion of wild flowers as it undulates along the cliff-tops. There are also many butterflies along this section which dart about in the gorse and brambles. A fence will join the path on the L.

After passing the numerous bays of Little Castle, Victoria and Watery Bay, you will reach the area of Gateholm Stack, where the path turns L to head ENE. You need to proceed as before, following the Coastal Path waymarkers. There are several P-stiles and the path weaves through a gap in a low wall, after which there are steep slopes of grass and sand to the R known as The Pits. These lie just to the N

of Raggle Rocks. A few steps further along the cliff-tops you will see a waymarker indicating a public footpath that leaves over a stile, due N. You should take this path (MR 778077), as it leads back to the car park. However, before doing so it is strongly recommended that you visit Marloes Sands, which lie just a short distance further along the Coastal Path. This beach is over 2km (1¼ miles) long and boasts a perfect combination of tall, rocky outcrops and smooth sands: just the place to bathe those tired feet before climbing back up to the return route.

Beyond the stile, the path heads inland on a dusty track to the R of a cornfield, near a fence. Away from the coastal breezes, this section of the route can be a suntrap. The path is straight and climbs gently towards an L-stile to the R of a metal gate. The route is waymarked here for the car park and you should follow the subsequent track to the R. This path is a little-used road that passes the youth hostel on the R. A short distance further on it leads to the car park to the L. With a little luck you will be able to relax with a choc-ice, as an ice-cream van is usually in attendance in summer!

Alternative routes

ESCAPES

It is possible to shorten this route by omitting the area of St Brides, instead joining the Coastal Path at Musselwick Sands. To do this you should turn L on the road just outside the village of Marloes, to head W for about 300 paces. The road climbs gradually towards Marloes Beacon, which is on the L, and a footpath leaves to the R. This descends over fields close to the boundary hedgerow, heading just E of N. After another 300 paces or so the path changes course to NW, following the boundary of the field and descending rapidly to join the Coastal Path near to Black Cliff. Turn L on to this and follow the route as previously described.

EXTENSIONS

Besides the small excursions to the Coast Guard Lookout and Marloes Sands, no further extensions are recommended.

155

Appendix: Relevant Addresses

This section provides a list of addresses that may be of use to walkers in Wales. It is not intended to be exhaustive and there are many sources of further information should it be required. The local Tourist Information Centre, National Park Authority or the National Trust can provide further details regarding accommodation and travel.

MOUNTAIN RESCUE SERVICE
999 EMERGENCY

SNOWDONIA NATIONAL PARK AUTHORITY

Tel (01766) 770274
Fax (01766) 771211

National Park Office
Penrhyndeudraeth
Gwynedd LL48 6LF

BRECON BEACONS NATIONAL PARK

Tel (01874) 624437
Fax (01874) 622574

National Park Office
7 Glamorgan Street
Brecon
Powys LD3 7DP

PEMBROKESHIRE COAST NATIONAL PARK DEPARTMENT

Tel (01437) 764591
Fax (01437) 769045

County Offices
St Thomas' Green
Haverfordwest
Pembrokeshire
Dyfed SA61 1QZ

Tourist Information Centres

denotes open seasonally April–September

Aberdyfi*	(01654) 767321
Wharf Gardens	
Aberdyfi	
Gwynedd LL35 0ED	

| Abersoch* | (01758) 712929 |
| Gwynedd LL53 7EA | |

Bala	(01678) 521021
Pensarn Road	
Bala	
Gwynedd LL23 7NH	

Bangor*	(01248) 352786
Llys y Gwynt	
Little Chef Complex	
A5/A55 Interchange	
Llandygai	
Bangor	
Gwynedd LL57 7BG	

Barmouth*	(01341) 280787
Old Library	
Station Road	
Barmouth	
Gwynedd LL42 1LU	

Betws-y-coed	(01690) 710426
Royal Oak Stables	
Betws-y-coed	
Gwynedd LL24 0AH	

Blaenau Ffestiniog* (01766) 830360
Isallt
High Street
Blaenau Ffestiniog
Gwynedd LL41 3HD

Caernarfon (01286) 672232
Oriel Pendeitsh
Castle Street
Caernarfon
Gwynedd LL55 2NA

Criccieth* (01766) 522850
High Street
Criccieth
Gwynedd LL52 0BS

Conwy (01492) 592248
Cadw Visitor Centre
Castle Entrance
Conwy
Gwynedd LL32 8LD

Corris* (01654) 761244
Craft Centre
Corris
Machynlleth
Gwynedd SY20 9SP

Dolgellau (01341) 422888
Eldon Square
Dolgellau
Gwynedd LL40 1PU

Harlech* (01766) 780658
Gwyddfor House
High Street
Harlech
Gwynedd LL46 1DR

Llanberis (01286) 870765
41a High Street
Llanberis
Gwynedd LL55 4UR

Llandudno (01492) 876413
1–2 Chapel Street
Llandudno
Gwynedd LL30 2SY

Porthmadog (01766) 512981 (24hr)
High Street
Porthmadog
Gwynedd LL49 9LD

Pwllheli (01758) 613000
Min y Don
Sqwar yr Orsaf
Pwllheli
Gwynedd LL53 5HG

Tywyn* (01654) 710070
High Street
Tywyn
Gwynedd LL36 9AD

Useful telephone numbers

Cadw – Welsh Historic Monuments (01222) 465511
Countryside Council for Wales (01248) 370444
Forestry Commission (01970) 612367
Mid-Wales Tourism (01654) 702653
Mountaincall (0891) 505330
National Rivers Authority (01222) 770088
National Trust (01492) 860123
North Wales Tourism (01492) 531731
North Wales Wildlife Trust (01248) 351541
Rambler's Association (01978) 855148
Wales Craft Council (01938) 555313
Wales Official Tourist Guides Association (01978)
    351212
Wales Tourist Board (01222) 499909
Weathercall (0891) 505315

Transport

For rail enquiries, the telephone number is 0345 484950.
Full bus timetable and fare information is available from
the relevant Tourist Information Office.

157

INDEX